INTERNATIONAL ENCYCLOPEDIA OF ART

European Art Since 1850

first edition

Nancy Malloy

Facts On File, Inc.

INTERNATIONAL ENCYCLOPEDIA OF ART
EUROPEAN ART SINCE 1850

*Cataloging-in-Publication Data available on request from
Facts On File, Inc.*

Facts on File books are available at special discounts when purchased in bulk quantities
for businesses, associations, institutions or sales promotions. Please call our
Special Sales Department in New York at 212/967-8800 or 800/322-8755.

This is a Mirabel Book produced by:
Cynthia Parzych Publishing, Inc.
648 Broadway
New York, NY 10012

**For my mother Ann who taught me how to see and for my son Tay
whose work makes seeing such a pleasure.**

Edited by: Frances Helby
Designed by: Dorchester Typesetting Group Ltd.
Printed and bound in Spain by: Imschoot Graphic Service

Front cover: Pierre-Auguste Renoir painted *Luncheon of the
Boating Party* in oil on canvas in 1881.

10 9 8 7 6 5 4 3 2 1

Contents

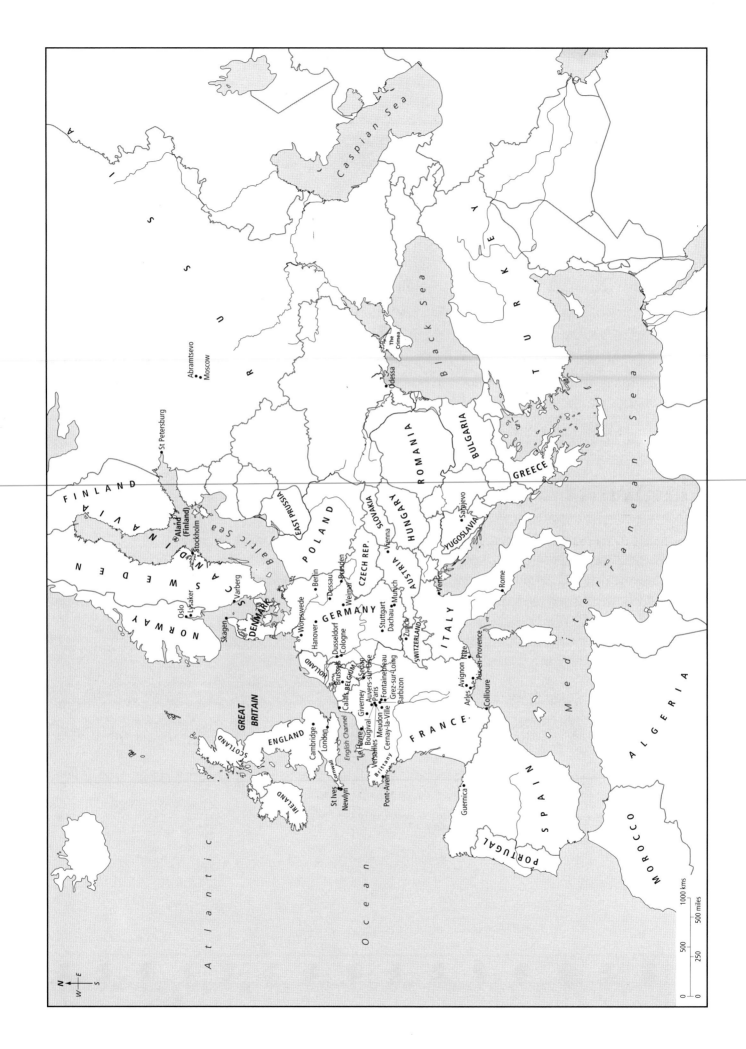

Introduction

Art is of its time. It is not a separate and isolated act but a function of the time and place in which it is made. Each art movement is a unique phenomenon of its historical period. Art generally reflects the social conditions, politics, and values of a society. Artists express their world in their work. The history of modern art in Europe covers the rich and exciting period from 1850 through the present. These were years full of change and progress. Through social unrest and political upheaval came an artistic revolution—a modern art.

Beginning in the mid-nineteenth century, revolution swept across Europe. In France, Italy, Germany and Austria, reforms were demanded and people took to the streets in open revolt. Artists were often in the forefront of the fight for change. Through their art they hoped to build a utopian world of higher understanding and achievement.

Modern art began as artists broke with tradition. Eugène Delacroix (1798–1863) challenged academic painting with his emotionally charged color paintings that launched Romanticism. It was here that the seeds of modernism were planted. The Realist painters, especially Gustave Courbet (1819–77), broke down the barriers of

Timeline

This timeline lists some of the important events, both historical (listed above the time bar) and art historical (below) that have been mentioned in this book. While every event cannot be mentioned it is hoped that this diagram will help the reader to understand at a glance how these events relate in time.

1851: The Great Exhibition is held in London.

1853: Baron von Haussman begins the reconstruction of Paris.

1859: Darwin publishes *The Origin of the Species by Means of Natural Selection*.

1850–1869 A.D.

1850s: The feud between Ingres and Delacroix is at its height. Foreign artists begin to join French artists' colonies. Realism is the dominant art style.

1857–60: The Arts and Crafts movement takes hold in England.

1870–71: The Franco–Prussian War.

1871: The Paris Commune survives for two months.

1870–mid-1880s A.D.

1870s: Artists' colonies flourish in Scandinavia.

1874: The first Impressionist exhibition is held.

1876: Cézanne arrives at his mature, revolutionary painting style.

1877: An artists' colony is founded at Abramtsevo in Russia.

1889: The Eiffel Tower is built for the Universal Exposition in Paris.

1894: Dreyfus is wrongly accused of espionage in France and his case becomes a *cause célèbre*.

1905: Demonstrations in St. Petersburg, Russia herald the approach of revolution. Einstein publishes his *Special Theory of Relativity*.

mid–1880s–1906 A.D.

mid–1880s: Pointillism and Divisionism develop and lead to Symbolism and Expressionism.

1898–1907: The Russian World of Art group makes Russia internationally important in the art world.

1904–06: Cézanne paints his most radical and influential works in the two years before his death.

1905: The Fauve and the Brücke groups are founded.

French society by painting ordinary people. By the latter part of the century, the Impressionists used new scientific theories of visual perception to create an art of color, light and sensations. They recorded contemporary scenes and are called the painters of modern life.

The twentieth century brought an explosion of ideas. New movements like Fauvism liberated color from its traditional role. Cubism broke all the rules of space and perspective and opened the door for a total break with the past: abstraction. The abstract painters and sculptors said that color and form alone could be the subject of a work of art. Through these elements, they could express feelings and emotion.

Einstein's scientific breakthroughs were felt by artists too. The world was becoming a different place in the early twentieth century. The railroad had given people mobility, modern machinery had given them more free time from the workplace, and the airplane gave them a glimpse of the future and a new concept of the world.

Artists tried to understand Einstein's "time-space" dimension theory and incorporate it in their work. The Russian avant-garde used this concept to create a new non-objective painting, called Suprematism, which did away with all representation and fixed viewpoints. Suprematist and Constructivist artists were both part of the Russian Revolution. They wanted to form a new society and believed that through their modern art and ideas they could do this. However, the new government soon became worried that these free-thinking creative people could be a threat to their

---

1907–17: Russia moves gradually towards revolution.

1914–18: World War I.

1915: Einstein publishes his *General Theory of Relativity*.

1917: The Russian Revolution begins.

1907–1918 A.D.

1907–09: Picasso's and Braque's work is the first phase of Cubism.

1908: The first Cubist exhibition is held.

1909: *Der Blaue Reiter* is founded in Germany. Futurism begins in Italy. In Russia, Constructivism and Suprematism become artistic responses to social and political unrest.

1910: Kandinsky paints the first abstract work.

1910–12: Cubism develops into its analytic phase.

1912–14: Cubism moves on to its synthetic phase.

1916: Dada begins in Zurich.

1919: The Versailles Treaty is signed, shaping post-war Europe.

1922: Mussolini forms a Fascist government in Italy.

1927: The German economy collapses.

1929: Wall Street crashes and economic depression begins worldwide.

1919–1929 A.D.

1917–19: Soviet artists use avant-garde art to further the Revolution.

1919: The Bauhaus is founded in Germany.

1922: Avant–garde art is banned in the Soviet Union.

1933: Hitler becomes Chancellor of Germany. All German political parties other than the Nazis are suspended.

1933–39: Germany rearms and begins to occupy territory outside its borders.

1936–39: The Spanish Civil War.

1930–1939 A.D.

1933: Modern art is suppressed in Germany. The Bauhaus is closed and some artists flee the country.

1937: Hitler holds an exhibition of "degenerate art" in Munich.

power and suppressed the production of the new art. This suppression would happen again in Nazi Germany where Adolf Hitler (1889–1945) burned books and banned modern art. The development of modern art required freedom to express oneself in an uninhibited way and the freedom to dismantle the past. It was therefore a threat to restrictive regimes which wanted complete control and dominance over the lives of their citizens.

After two devastating world wars, Europe found itself divided into two political camps. The Cold War pitted the democratic nations of the west against the Communist nations of eastern Europe. Artists in the Communist-controlled countries were forbidden to make modern art. The state-sanctioned art was one of social realism showing happy workers and peasants in the service of the nation. Nevertheless, many artists engaged in the underground production of modern art that would surface when Communism was dismantled. In the west, abstraction was challenged in the late 1950s by Pop Art. Pop artists found their ideas and inspiration in popular culture and mass media images. They were soon challenged by Minimal and Conceptual artists.

Installation Art uses mixed media—painting, sculpture, video, music and lasers. It is an art of involvement and interaction. It can also be a personal exploration, a comment on society or it can become a political arena.

Artists can be thought of as the reporters of the time in which they live. Artists are often in the vanguard of ideas for change. Art, culture and politics are often closely bound together.

1939–45: World War II.

1939–1945 A.D.

1940s: The art capital of the world begins to shift to New York. Many artists remain in wartorn Europe.

1941: Henry Moore draws people sheltering from the Blitz in the London subway.

1945: Europe begins a program of post-war reconstruction. The Cold War between the west and the Soviet bloc begins and lasts for more than forty years.

1945–1980 A.D.

1949: The first Art Brut exhibition is held.

1950s: Pop Art emerges alongside Conceptual art.

mid–1960s: Op Art develops.

late 1960s: Situationist, Performance, Installation, Environmental and Kinetic art and *Arte Povera* develop.

late 1980s: The Communist world begins to disintegrate.

1989: The Berlin Wall is demolished and the Cold War ends.

1990: The Soviet Union is abolished and Germany is reunited.

1991: War breaks out in the Balkans.

1992: The Gulf War is fought.

1980s–present

late 1980s–90s: European art, particularly in Germany, recovers its confidence and Postmodern Neo-expressionism develops. The media plays an important part in art.

1 Seeds of Modernism

Revolutions of 1848

In January 1848 a rebellion broke out in Sicily sparked by a local conflict and spread throughout the kingdom of Naples. In February Paris became the scene of street riots that led to the proclamation of the Second Republic. Someone said, "When Paris sneezed, Europe caught cold," for trouble in Paris caused a chain-reaction of social and political revolution all over Europe. Germany, Italy, Hungary, Croatia and Bohemia all saw uprisings and change. Hardly a government in Europe was left unshaken by the the end of 1848. ■

Throughout the nineteenth century, Europe experienced great changes in its politics and basic social structure. By mid-century, revolutions were taking place in France, Germany, Austria and Italy. People throughout Europe were demanding broad social and political reforms. At this time, most Europeans lived in the country and in small towns, but with the rise of industrialization, new methods of transportation and a significant increase in the population, people were making the shift from a rural lifestyle to an urban one. They sought employment in the cities, but living and working conditions for the lower classes were bad. This created a climate of dissatisfaction and unrest.

In Paris, thousands were living in the city in unbelievable squalor and working under terrible conditions in 1848. Lack of sanitation and overcrowding led to a deadly cholera epidemic which claimed many lives. Added to this was an unsteady economy and a credit collapse, resulting in widespread unemployment. The seeds of revolution

Haussmann's wide boulevards, this one radiating from Paris's Arc de Triumphe, were planned to allow the cavalry to charge potential rioters and to allow for a good line of fire if trouble erupted in the streets of Paris. ▼

A Plan for Paris

In 1853, Baron Georges Eugène Haussmann began restructuring the city of Paris. He laid out beautiful, wide boulevards, a new sewer system, and tree-lined streets with parks ringing the city, providing recreation for the newly emerging middle class, the bourgeoisie. New industries had created a social class which had more money and more leisure time. Haussmann's plans did beautify the great city, but there was also an underlying political plan at work. The 1848 revolt had been caused in part by a response to the cholera outbreak, so the building of a new sewer system protected the government from further criticism or responsibility. The grand boulevards allowed for easy monitoring by the police in case of riot and the wide avenues would also allow cavalry to charge against rioters if there was full-scale fighting. Haussmann displaced 350,000 working-class and poor people from the inner city to the outskirts of Paris. He envisioned a city with new living quarters and recreational spaces for the bourgeoisie. Here, they could walk along the broad boulevards, stroll through the parks, and frequent the brightly lit cafes on the main streets. While Haussmann's plan was forward thinking in its program to modernize Paris, provide good living conditions, recreation and convenience for the middle class, there was little concern for the lower classes. ■

▲ Paganini, *approx. 1832, by Eugène Delacroix, is an emotional oil on canvas work.*

Ingres's pencil drawing of his friend, the famed violinist, Paganini, *1819, is a factual, emotionless portrait.* ▼

were sown. Artists too were in revolt, throwing out tradition and searching for new ways to express themselves in a rapidly changing world. They wanted to create an "art of their own time, a modern art."

By the nineteenth century, the older empires of Spain, Portugal and Holland were in decline. France and Great Britain had become the major powers in Europe and were expanding their empires around the globe. By 1850, England was the center of manufacturing and industry and Paris was the center of the art world. Within a few years Baron Georges Eugène Haussmann (1809–91) would undertake the restructuring of Paris, making it a model for the modern city and also establishing it as the undisputed cultural center of the world.

Progress was the driving force in the mid-1800s and the concept of the new took on great importance. Revolution had brought change. Change had come to artists, too. Once dependent solely upon the patronage of the nobility and the church, they were now more independent. The state and the national academies controlled the art market. The middle class had money to buy art but not the education to fully understand the art they bought. Art critics became important sources of expertise. Established painters and sculptors showed their work at annual Salons sponsored by the state and the academies. This

The Feud _____

A highly publicized feud between the painters Ingres and Delacroix broke out in 1824 Ingres was a Neo-Classicist who worked with a restrained but elegant palette and relied on line to construct his paintings. The Romantic painter Delacroix found his expression through rich color, charged with feeling and imagination.

The feud split France's contemporary artists. Academic painters, on the side of Ingres declared that only through line was the artist's truthfulness revealed. The younger, modern artists believed in Delacroix's expressive use of

▲ *The feud between Ingres and Delacroix was so heated that cartoons were published showing them like knights in battle. Delacroix's shield reads, "Line is color!" while Ingres's states, "Color is Utopia. Long live line!"*

color. Heated debates and articles continued to recount the clash of ideas that finally ended in 1857. ■

Eugène Delacroix's exciting oil on canvas ▶ The Tiger Hunt, 1854, in which he depicts man against beast, recalls his trip to North Africa. The sights and colors of Morocco greatly influenced his work. It is a work full of drama and emotion.

The Great Exhibition of 1851_____

The Great Exhibition of the Works of Industry of All Nations held in London in 1851 brought together the marvels of mid-nineteenth century technology and industry in Great Britain and Europe. Since Great Britain was the most technically advanced country, it assumed the leading role. The organizers hoped that the fair would stimulate trade, be educational and appeal to all classes. No paintings were exhibited but some examples of sculpture and a few architectural models were shown.

The architect Joseph Paxton (1801–65) was hired to create a building that would highlight the advances made in construction. It was a great glass and iron structure. The magazine *Punch* in its November 2, 1850, issue called the building "the Crystal Palace," and the name stuck. It was built in Hyde Park in central London.

Paxton used 293,655 panes of glass and 4,500 tons of iron. It housed 7,381 British exhibitors and over 6,000 foreign ones. The average attendance per day was over 42,000 visitors. The exhibition was a tremendous success. ∎

guaranteed them respectability and a professional living. However, the younger artists were not accepted into the official Salons.

In this climate of change and upheaval a new movement emerged, Romanticism, the start of a modern art style. Romanticism rejected rational thought in favor of feelings, putting emotions above everything else. The German artist Casper David Friedrich (1774–1840) was the first Romantic painter but, in France, Eugène Delacroix would embrace the style and make it his own. He broke with tradition and produced work filled with emotion and expressiveness generated by rich color and strong brushwork. Delacroix brought art into the modern realm through his painting, color theories and writings. His work and theories had a great influence on the Impressionists and other modern artists in the early twentieth century.

Delacroix's visit to North Africa in 1832 changed his life. The light and colors of Morocco were totally different from the European land-

The large glass and iron building called the ▶ Crystal Palace was built for the Great Exhibition of 1851 held in London. Joseph Paxton's impressive design was one of the marvels of nineteenth century technology.

▲ *This early photograph by William Henry Fox Talbot,* A View of the Boulevards of Paris, 1843, *shows the careful detail that the first cameras were able to capture.*

Daguerreotypes

L.J.M. Daguerre developed the first practical photographic process in 1837. His early photographs show that his camera could capture minute detail and give a full range of tones from black to white. After his collaborator J.N. Nièpce's (1765–1833) death Daguerre developed a process to fix images on a silvered copper plate to create a daguerreotype. This was a breakthrough for photography and became the most widely used process at the time. ■

▲ *The range of tones that the daguerreotype process was able to achieve is seen in the print,* Still Life in Studio, 1837, *photographed by Daguerre showing the interior of his studio.*

scape. The rich colors and Arab dress offered the artist a new way of looking at things. Delacroix was also influenced by the English painter John Constable (1776–1837). Constable's work showed that the landscape was filled with different shades of greens and blues and reflections. Delacroix built on this knowledge to produce a romantic vision of the world.

The leading painter of the day in France was Neo-Classicist Jean Auguste Dominique Ingres (1780–1867) who called Delacroix the "apostle of the ugly." By ugly he meant any art that broke with tradition and was modern. Ingres's work was extremely rational, formal and detached. He used subdued color and his paintings were linear rather than colorful and painterly. His beautiful use of line and formal, compositional arrangements created pictures in a classic style. He showed objects as he observed them. The Romantic painters, on the other hand, painted objects with an emphasis on their own expressive imaginations.

After the Great Exhibition of 1851 in Great Britain, France decided to mount its own Universal Exposition in 1889 in Paris. Unable to compete with Great Britain in manufacturing, France decided to concentrate on the arts and sciences.

In England, the Arts and Crafts movement developed between 1857 and 1860. Designers William Morris (1834–96) and Philip Webb (1831–1915) created wallpaper, furniture, tapestries and rugs with the same care as fine artists took with a painting or sculpture. The Arts and Crafts movement started as a protest against manufactured goods. Its followers emulated the medieval artisan guilds that had produced finely crafted goods made by hand. The Victorian era in England also saw a return to the Gothic and pre-Renaissance artistry in architecture, decorative arts and painting, with the Pre-Raphaelite Brotherhood, who looked for inspiration in previous centuries.

One of the most important discoveries during this time was photography. In England, photographer W.H. Fox Talbot (1800–77) developed the negative to positive process of photography in the late 1830s. His book, *The Pencil of Nature*, was published in 1844 with a second volume in 1846. It contained twenty-four mounted photographs and an accompanying text. At the same time in France, Hippolyte Bayard (1801–87) took pictures of Montmartre and its environs. Bayard was the first photographer to exhibit his pictures in public in July 1839. However, his progress was soon overshadowed by L.J.M. Daguerre (1789–1851) whose process became the most effective in producing good quality pictures. Painters became fascinated with the new technique and quickly began to use photography to provide models for their paintings. Many painters became photographers themselves.

2 The Politics of Realism

Marxism and Society

Karl Marx (1818–83) was a German philosopher. He and his collaborator Friedrich Engels (1820–95) analyzed social conditions in nineteenth-century Europe. They came to the conclusion that capitalism exploited workers and that no equality could be achieved within this system. Marxism, they believed, offered equality to all members of society. Their *Communist Manifesto* was published in 1848. It called for workers to unite and for the formation of a classless society. Their ideas were the foundation for the Russian Revolution of 1917.

In practice, the Marxist philosophy led to authoritarian government which restricted freedom for the masses. Repression of liberties was considered a necessary measure to maintain control. Nevertheless, Marxist ideas resonated in democratic societies which also had to struggle with issues of equality. ■

▲ *Karl Marx lent his name to a system of socialism that was looked at as a religion by some people. He is pictured here with his wife.*

▲ *Rosa Bonheur was interested in exploring the realism of daily events. She romanticized them with her daring painting style. This is her oil on canvas,* Plowing in the Niverais: The Dressing of the Vines *of 1849.*

Realism examined the daily life of ordinary people. It recorded everyday events: workers in the city, peasants in the fields, people on trains, mourners at a small town funeral and local people attending services at a village church. The common tasks of workers and the treatment of the poor were important images that Realist artists used to look at their society. They wanted to record exactly what they saw. They were interested in truth: the depiction of how things really are in the world. It was an important exploration undertaken by both writers and artists in the nineteenth century.

Rosa Bonheur (1822–99) was an artist who strove for realism. Her painting, *Plowing in the Nivernais: The Dressing of the Vines*, 1849 records with detailed realism the agricultural practices of this French region. Bonheur's rendering of anatomy is extremely accurate. She spent many hours in slaughterhouses throughout Paris carefully analyzing the bones and muscle structure of animals. Standing in blood and entrails, Bonheur would make her careful drawings. She dressed in trousers and jacket, like a man, in order to move about without hindrance. Like the female writer, George Sand (1804–76), whom she greatly admired, Bonheur adopted a style of dress that made her equal to her male counterparts.

Rosa Bonheur was one of the most successful painters of the nineteenth century. The naturalism of her paintings and the individuality of their execution made her a favorite artist of the time. Her father, Raimond Bonheur, was an artist who taught drawing and tutored his daughter. He and his family were members of a group called the

▲ *The overtly political art of Honoré Daumier shows the bodies of murdered tenants in a working class area of Paris. This lithograph is entitled,* Rue Transnonain, *1834.*

Call for Social Reform

In order to have her work published and to be taken seriously as a writer, Mary Ann Evans (1819–80) took the pen name of George Eliot. Her books were chronicles of domestic realism. *Adam Bede* published in 1859 was received with great enthusiasm. It established her as a leading writer in England. Her readers speculated that George Eliot was either a clergyman or the wife of a clergyman.

Silas Marner was published in 1861 and Eliot's reputation was secured. With the publication of *Middlemarch* in installments in 1871 and 1872, Eliot's commitment to social reform was well documented. *Middlemarch*, a study of provincial life in a small town in rural England, explores the role of women, the politics of the day and the clearly defined class divisions. Through her characters, Eliot analyzed the political upheavals of the time. She called for social reforms. In 1919, writer Virginia Woolf (1882–1941) said that *Middlemarch* was one of the few English novels written for grown-ups. ■

This large Realist, oil on canvas, entitled, ▶
The Stonebreakers, *1849, by Gustave Courbet, outraged the public when first shown. Realists believed in painting life as they saw it.*

Saint-Simonian Community which believed in the equality of women. The group felt that women were here to elevate the human race. Bonheur's family and the community supported her in her pursuit of an art career. She won the first medal in the Paris Salon of 1853 with her painting entitled *The Horse Fair* and was made an Officer of the Legion of Honor, a prestigious award. The painting was reproduced in an engraving and distributed throughout Europe.

The work of Realists like Honoré Daumier, Jean François Millet and Gustave Courbet challenged inequalities in society. Honoré Daumier (1808–79) attacked the government and the living and working conditions endured by the lower classes. Through lithographic prints and published cartoons, he produced biting satire questioning the whole social fabric of France during this period. The murder scene in his *Rue Transnonain*, 1834, shows working-class people, slaughtered in their night clothes. They were merely under suspicion of having fired on government troops. It was a strong indictment of the regime and a powerful protest against injustice.

The greatest Realist painter was Gustave Courbet (1819–77) whose work revolutionized art at the time and had a tremendous influence on artists for generations. Courbet painted ordinary people in the countryside and in his Parisian studio, not only recording events as he saw them but challenging the class structure and the privilege accorded to the rich.

When Courbet painted *The Stonebreakers*, 1849, which was destroyed in World War II, nineteenth century patrons of the arts were used to seeing workers depicted as heroic laborers, idealized as victims of their jobs, not society. But, here Courbet painted a man and boy working by the roadside breaking stones, their backs turned towards the viewer in an indifferent gesture. The public was outraged, they felt this indifference was an insult to them. The large canvas

When Gustave ▶ Courbet decided to paint A Burial at Ornans *in 1849, he asked fifty-one local people to gather in the village's new cemetery so he could paint each character from life. Among the cast of characters are members of Courbet's family and the town's mayor.*

Nadar always attempted to reflect the inner, active character of his subject through the face. Among the many leading figures in the arts photographed by Nadar was the great actress Sarah Bernhardt, 1859. Bernhardt was said to have kept a coffin at the foot of her bed. She outraged the public by performing on stage as Hamlet, a man, in William Shakespeare's play. ▼

showed the laborers without apology. The subject matter was thought to be inappropriate for such a monumental work because such epic paintings generally had historical subjects. In another canvas, *Burial at Ornans*, 1849, Courbet showed a village funeral marking the death of an ordinary man. In the painting the funeral becomes a testament to everyman in every small village.

Although Courbet tried to present a truthful portrayal of what he saw, he did embellish the truth with his own ideas. Jean François Millet (1814–75) did this too. Millet went to the village of Barbizon in the forest of Fontainebleau not far from Paris to paint. He stayed for years painting peasants at work in the fields. He idealized the

Portraits of Parisian Life

The photographer Gaspard-Félix Tournachon (1820–1910) changed his name in 1849 to Nadar. Between 1852 and 1870, he photographed many famous actors, artists and literary figures in Paris. Nadar grasped the immediacy of the moment in his work and tried to capture the active lives of his subjects. His photographs captured people in passing, caught in the fleeting moment. This sense of time was a preoccupation of Modernism. Nadar even took his camera up in a hot-air balloon to take aerial views in 1856. He had worked as a journalist in Paris in the early 1840s and wrote for left-wing publications. He was a bohemian and lived in the Latin Quarter of Paris where he was under police surveillance for his political beliefs and activities. In 1852, he published *Pantheon Nadar*, a lithographed sheet of 300 caricatures, some photographs, of his Parisian literary contemporaries. He photographed Manet, Courbet, Daumier, Baudelaire and the famous actress, Sarah Bernhardt, among others. ■

Photography as Fine Art

English photographer, Julia Margaret Cameron (1815–79), took photographs that seem to transport her subjects to a dreamier, more imaginative realm. She was not interested in the transient or the immediacy of a subject, but in its poetic aspects. She counted among her artist and poet friends the Pre-Raphaelite painter Dante Gabriel Rossetti and the poet, Alfred, Lord Tennyson. Her portrait of Mrs. Duckworth, approx. 1867, is a soft-focus picture that gives a poetic look to her subject. Cameron's figures emerge from the darkness. They seem to be portraits of the inner life of the mind and spirit of Cameron's subject. Cameron tried to bring photography into the sphere of high art. ■

Julia Margaret Cameron's portrait of Mrs. Herbert Duckworth, shows ▶ *the mother of writer Virginia Woolf who was part of the Bloomsbury Group that challenged Victorian conventions.*

▲ *The German Realist movement was led by Wilhelm Leibl whose oil on canvas* Three Women in a Village Church, *1878–81, shows three generations of women at mass in a local church. The beautifully composed picture is direct and meticulously detailed.*

peasants doing their daily labor. They did not complain, but complacently did their jobs. The scenes become pastoral rather than a political indictment of the semi-feudal agricultural system.

Realist painting was also being done in Germany by Wilhelm Leibl (1844–1900). Leibl's intricately detailed work realistically captured the people he painted in rural Germany. In *Three Women in a Village Church*, 1878-81, Leibl showed three generations of peasant women at mass, praying and listening attentively in their pew. It is its directness and simplicity that make it such a strong portrait.

Evolution and Charles Darwin

The English naturalist Charles Darwin (1809–82) published *The Origin of the Species by Means of Natural Selection*, in 1859. His theories began to take shape on a voyage surveying the coast of South America in 1831 on the ship *Beagle*. Another naturalist, Alfred Russell Wallace (1823–1913) was exploring ideas similar to Darwin's and they presented a joint paper in 1858 in London. Darwin's scientific studies came to the conclusion that life on earth had evolved by natural selection. "Social Darwinism" was a late nineteenth century movement that used Darwin's theory as an excuse for doing nothing about bad social conditions. It justified keeping the lower classes and the poor where they were because they had not evolved as far as the ruling class. Social Darwinism was discredited in the early twentieth century as people realized that some faced economic disadvantages and were not born inferior. ■

3   The Painting of Modern Life

Impression Sunrise, 1872, *painted in oil on* ▶
*canvas by Claude Monet, inspired the name of
the group of painters who exhibited in the first
Impressionist exhibition in 1874. The scene
is an impression of the foggy harbor at
Le Havre in Normandy.*

Salon des Refusés

A harsh jury rejected three-fifths of the almost 4,000 works of art entered in the official Salon of 1863. Most artists were angry. Napoleon III wanted to be fair and liberal on this issue, so he asked to see the rejected works. He pronounced the rejected work as good as the pieces accepted by the jury. He ordered another exhibition, a *Salon des Refusés*, to be held at the Palais de l'Industrie nearby. It opened on May 11, 1863, and more than 7,000 visitors came on the first day. Works by Manet, Pissarro, Cézanne, Fantin-Latour, Boudin, Jongkind and Whistler were shown. ∎

*Camille Pissarro, the "Father of
Impressionism" painted* Place du Théâtre
Français *in 1895 in oil on canvas. It gives an
impression of a busy street scene with the
people and carriages carefully sketched.* ▼

With the surrender of the French armies at Sedan in northeast France in September 1870, the Franco-Prussian War came to a climax with a crushing defeat for Napoleon III. He was forced to abdicate, leaving a provisional government in Versailles, just outside Paris. Paris was under siege for months but held out against the Prussians. The French provisional government wanted to end the war and ordered the Paris National Guard to surrender their arms but they would not. The Paris Commune was formed and established its own governing body. War was declared on the Versailles government.

A number of artists were involved in the Commune: Gustave Courbet was named Curator of Fine Arts, Edouard Manet was a member, and the most active participant was Camille Pissarro. The bloody climax occurred on May 28, 1871, just seventy-two days after it had begun. The police killed 20,000 men, women and children as they took down barricades. Women were particularly singled out for brutality. The *Communards* fought to the end, unwilling to settle for anything less than freedom.

Out of this political turmoil came another kind of revolution, an artistic one called Impressionism. It began with Pissarro, Monet and others who painted outdoors in the sunlight. This *plein air* painting was spearheaded by Camille Pissarro (1830–1903), who was called the "Father of Impressionism."

Impressionist painters recorded the sensations of light and color

▲ Rouen Cathedral, (Full Sunlight), *1894, is one of Monet's forty oil on canvas explorations of the effects of light, weather conditions and the changing seasons on the building.*

Claude Monet _____

Claude Monet (1840–1926) painted many series in his lifetime. His work had the greatest impact on the new Impressionist painting. He rented a room overlooking the west porch of Rouen Cathedral. He painted forty versions of the cathedral between 1893 and 1895. He sometimes worked on fourteen canvases at a time. The building was changed by the light and weather conditions that altered its surface so that it looked different on each canvas. The experiments of Monet and the other Impressionists used color for shadows and pure color to show light variations. ■

that they experienced first-hand in the open air. They wanted to paint modern life objectively by rendering an "impression" of what they saw. Influenced by the optical theories of Michel Eugène Chevreul (1786–1889) and the advances made in photography, many of the Impressionists put the feathery effects created by the camera into their paintings. They also experimented with color associations. A new sense of light was achieved in their work as they painted on white canvases instead of color grounds. This allowed a shimmering light to come through the rich color.

The Impressionists refused to paint historical or idealized scenes that academic painters produced; they wanted to paint modern life, in a modern way. They captured the fleeting moment as they recorded different colors and the special light of each time of the day and of each season. They captured effects as they quickly changed, recording moments that can never recur.

Many of the artists worked side by side in the open air, experimenting and sharing ideas. Monet, Sisley and Renoir all worked together in Fontainebleau, not far from Paris, in 1864, creating soft focus impressions of the landscape. In 1869, Claude Monet and Auguste Renoir (1841–1919) painted together just west of Paris at a beauty spot called La Grenouillère creating pictures of the harbor at Bougival. They experimented with light and shadow, discovering that shadows were not brown and black but were really colors tinted by the surrounding colors. Light unified figures and landscape. These early experiments in painting led the Impressionists to band together for exhibitions since the official Salon would not show their work.

The Impressionists' first exhibition opened on April 15, 1874, and was held in the studio which the photographer Nadar had recently vacated. It was on the boulevard des Capucines and the rue Damou, where many Impressionists had painted the busy street. A total of thirty artists exhibited their work, including Pissarro and his student Cézanne, Degas, Renoir and Morisot.

Claude Monet ▶ dressed in his best clothes and went to the Gare St. Lazare, the title of this 1877 oil on canvas. Thinking he was a successful Salon artist, a railroad official cleared the platform and had the engines let off steam.

The Sculptor Rodin

Auguste Rodin (1840–1917) is considered the greatest sculptor of the beginning of the modern era. His work is very expressive and incorporates a strong realism. He went to Italy in 1875 to study and was impressed by the work of Michelangelo Buonarroti (1475–1564) whose influence is obvious in his work. At the same time, Rodin used the Impressionists' idea of capturing the fleeting moment. This sense of a moment caught in time leads sculpture right into the twentieth century.

During his career, Rodin produced an immense amount of work. *The Thinker* (1880), *The Kiss* (1886) and the large grouping of medieval leaders of the town of Calais, entitled *The Burghers of Calais* (1884-86) are among his best known works.

By 1900, Rodin's reputation as the greatest living sculptor of his time was established. The year before Rodin died, he bequeathed his work to the French nation. ■

The great ▶ French writer Balzac was honored by sculptor Auguste Rodin in his bronze Monument to Balzac, *1897. When it was first exhibited, it caused a riot because of its modern, dramatic pose.*

◀ *The subject of Berthe Morisot's 1869–70 oil on canvas* The Mother and Sister of the Artist, *was a subject that fell within the boundaries restricting women artists in the late 1800s.*

Berthe Morisot (1841–95) became a close friend of Manet's and later married his brother Eugène. She was a fine painter and resented the fact that because she was a woman she was restricted as an artist. She called it "the injustice of fate." Edouard Manet (1832–83), the unofficial leader of the group, was represented as was Monet, whose painting, *Impression Sunrise*, gave the group its name. Critic Louis Leroy used "Impressionism" as a term of disapproval in his review. Both he and the public criticized the show harshly.

Edouard Manet had replaced Courbet as the inspiration for the young avant-garde. He was wealthy, educated and a liberal. He attacked Napoleon III in his work, *The Death of Maximillian*. He also painted and drew scenes of the daily atrocities committed by the troops of the Versailles government and the police against the Paris Commune.

Edgar Degas (1834–1917) shared Manet's upper-class background. They were both somewhat separated from the Impressionists by their social class, education, age and especially their artistic aims. Manet and Degas never lost sight of form and structure in their work. They never reduced their brushstrokes to impresssionistic dabs of color

Degas was very interested in Japanese art and his use of strong diagonals, bird's-eye views and unique perspectives shows the influence of the *ukiyo-e* artists he admired. He produced candid scenes of women bathing, dancers, the theater, racetracks and Parisian cafes using beautiful line and color and often exploring the effects of artificial light. Degas exhibited with the Impressionists, but he denied

▲ *Edgar Degas was fascinated by the world of dance and theater. The effects of artificial light and the candid views of off-stage performers in* Ballet Rehearsal (Adagio), *1876, painted in oil on canvas, offers a glimpse of theatrical life not seen before. Degas uses the strong diagonal and different point of view of Japanese art.*

Mary Cassatt's tender oil on canvas portrait of a mother and child in The Bath *(about 1892), shows the influence Japanese art also had on her work.* ▼

being one. His close friend, the American Mary Cassatt (1844–1926), also exhibited with the group after she had been rejected by both the 1875 and 1877 Salons. Cassatt and the other female Impressionists, painted the private world of the home and family. Social custom did not allow women to paint outdoors and in the cafes of the city.

The Impressionists painted people with leisure time, the new class of consumers. They celebrated modernity. Paris was the city of power, culture and progress and the Impressionists responded to this in their images of everyday life.

Altogether, there were eight Impressionist exhibitions held from 1874 to 1886. By the last exhibition, Impressionism had been accepted and the Impressionists, at first ridiculed, were now the leading

In Pierre- ▶
Auguste Renoir's,
Luncheon of the
Boating Party,
1881, painted in oil on canvas, the artist shows the effects of sunlight pouring through the trees onto the party goers.

painters of the time. Their influence spread throughout Europe and to America as artists adopted this new and modern style. In music too, the Impressionist influence took root in the work of Claude Debussy (1862–1918). His music was built up of tones that created a continuous form. Impressionism had a tremendous impact on developments in art in the twentieth century.

Japonisme

Japanese prints were an important source of inspiration for the Impressionists. The *ukiyo-e* prints, "pictures of the floating world," showed everyday contemporary life in Japan. They used unique perspectives, close-ups, cropped views and images of modern life.

Many artists also used oriental subjects in their paintings as exotic props, but it was artists like Degas and van Gogh who used the asymmetrical compositional style of Japanese art to create something new. ■

4 Working Together

▲ *This photograph of a* Masked Ball at Grez, France *approx. 1880, shows the bohemian social life of the artists.*

A Russian Colony

▲ *This is a photograph of* The Mamontovs Dining at Abramtsevo *taken in the 1880s.*

Thirty miles/nearly fifty kilometers north of Moscow is Abramtsevo, an artists' colony founded in 1877 on the summer estate of railroad tycoon Savva Mamontov and his wife Elizabeth. Mamontov welcomed writers, musicians and artists to stay and made Abramtsevo an important art colony. ■

With growing interest in outdoor painting in the nineteenth century, artists sought out new, fresh places to paint where they could live cheaply and share the camaraderie of other artists. Artists' colonies sprang up throughout Europe. Each summer, artists from many countries met, worked together, and enjoyed each other's company.

The artists worked hard on their paintings, often studying with better known artists during the day, and later meeting in local cafes to talk and argue about their work. Many women artists came to these colonies because social barriers there were relaxed.

One of the most important art colonies was located at Barbizon in the forest of Fontainebleau, southeast of Paris, in France. Camille Corot (1796–1875) and several of his young followers had visited and worked there. Theodore Rousseau (1812–67) began painting there about 1827. Charles-François Daubigny (1817–78) and Jean-François Millet arrived there in 1849. Millet, who became one of the most famous Barbizon painters, settled there permanently.

By mid-century, Barbizon's fame had spread outside France and many artists came to work there including Karl Bodmer (1805–93), from Switzerland, who remained until his death. *A Guide to the Forest of Fontainebleau* was published and brought tourists by the hundreds to look at the beautiful scenery and at the bohemian artists. Now, overrun with tourists and artists, some painters sought refuge in the nearby village of Grez-sur-Loing. Other artists went to Cernay-la-Ville, southwest of Paris.

The Boyarina Morosova, *1881–87, was painted in oil on canvas, by Vassily Surikov a member of The Wanderers who worked at Abramtsevo.* ▼

Rise of Railroads

The public railroad system opened in England in 1825 making transportation from London to neighboring towns accessible. Railway lines in Europe could support trains that could go up to speeds of 100 miles/about 160 kilometers per hour. This helped move products from one city to the next very quickly. Around 1850 railroad lines were laid in France, connecting Paris to the nearby country-side. Not only was transportation a major factor in creating new industries, it also provided access to new places for recreation. Trains carried people away for a Sunday afternoon or weekend of fun in the country. Artists could find new landscapes to paint in the open air a short ride from their city studios. ■

▲ *This photograph of* Artists in Front of the Pension Gloanec, Pont-Aven, *approx. 1880, shows a group of Pont-Aven artists meeting at a popular inn after a day of painting.*

Paul Gauguin was fascinated by the customs and traditional dress of the Breton people. One traditional event held over a three or four day period included wrestling matches. Gauguin's 1888 oil on canvas, Vision After the Sermon, Jacob Wrestling with the Angel, *records this event. The unusual headdresses of the Breton women watching the match are in the foreground.* ▼

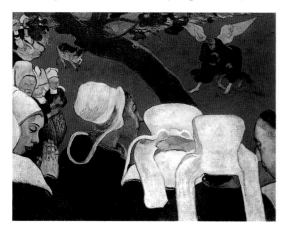

A large group of Scandinavian artists came to Grez because of the renowned French painter Jules Bastien-Lepage (1848–84) who they greatly admired. By 1882, painters from Norway included Christian Skredsvig and Christian Krohg (1852–1925). Carl Larsson (1853–1919) from Sweden also arrived. A substantial number of women artists arrived at this time including Julia Beck and Emma Lowstadt. Some even married members of the colony.

Barbizon's fame declined as Grez became more popular. However, it was Pont-Aven, also in France, that in the 1870s, attracted the most artists. Pont-Aven was even more remote. Here in Brittany, the locals looked exotic in their large hats and colorful costumes. The Bretons are a Celtic people, many of whose ancestors originally migrated from England centuries ago to escape the Anglo-Saxon invasion. They fiercely retained their customs, dress and independent spirit. They were devout Catholics and held week-long religious rituals each year which the artists eagerly attended. The Bretons fascinated Paul Gauguin (1848–1903) who arrived in Pont-Aven in the late 1880s. The colony was a favorite with Danish artists and since Gauguin was married to a Danish woman, he had ties there.

Gauguin headed what was called the Nabis group with Emile Bernard, Pierre Bonnard and Maurice Denis, using wonderful flat areas of color in their paintings which rejected naturalistic representation.

Large numbers of Scandinavians went to art colonies in France because their countries were political allies of France. Germany, which had been their traditional training ground, was now hostile. The Swedish king, Karl XV, himself an artist, called on Swedes to

▲ *This lively painting of artists at the local inn in Skagen is called* Artists' Breakfast. *P.S. Krøyer painted this scene in oil on canvas in 1883 showing the group in an animated conversation before going off to paint for the day.*

boycott the German academies and to study in France. However, by the 1880s, Scandinavian countries had established art colonies in their own countries. Gauguin's brother-in-law, Frits Thaulow (1847–1906) founded the first *plein air* academy in Modum, Norway. He worked with the effects of weather on the landscape in his paintings. In Finland, a colony was established at Aland and in Sweden at Varberg, the painters Richard Bergh (1858–1919) and Nils Kreuger formed a colony in 1892. But, it was in Denmark, at Skagen, that the largest and most successful colony was established. Peder Severin Krøyer (1851–1909), who had worked at Grez, went there and painted the local fishermen. He stayed there until his death. Mathias Rorbye, however, was the first artist to come to Skagen in 1833. Krøyer, Thaulow and Krohg were now the main artists there. In 1859, writer Hans Christian Andersen (1805–75) visited Skagen and wrote *Tales of the Dunes* there.

In the 1870s, Munich was the main art center in Germany and artists formed a group called Leibl's Circle around Realist artist Wilhelm Leibl (1844–1900). A large colony at Dachau, near Munich, flourished between the 1850s and the 1880s. *Plein air* painting was so popular that Kaiser Wilhelm II lectured against it, imploring German artists to follow the tradition of heroic painting instead. A new colony eventually emerged in the town of Worpswede, near Bremen, in northwestern Germany.

John Ruskin and the Pre-Raphaelite Brotherhood

John Ruskin (1819–1900) was the leading art critic of his time. Through his writing, Ruskin attempted to shape British public taste and to create a national art. In *Modern Painters*, published between 1834 and 1860, he denounced "greed as a deadly principle guiding English life." He called for a return to the past, to medieval values and craftsmanship, to recapture its heroic and Christian social ideals.

The painters of the Pre-Raphaelite Botherhood also looked back in time for inspiration. The Brotherhood was formed in 1848 by John Everett Millais, Dante Gabriel Rossetti and William Holman Hunt. They used Realism to paint images from literature, historical events and fantasy. ■

▲ Ophelia, *painted in oil on canvas in 1852 makes the viewer believe that John Everett Millais witnessed Shakespeare's character's death.*

▲ *This photograph shows the studio at the* Art School at St. Ives, *around 1900.*

▲ *This is Stanhope Forbes's oil on canvas of 1885,* The Fish Sale.

Bloomsbury Group ___

The Bloomsbury Group was made up of artists, intellectuals and literary figures centered at the home of writer Virginia Woolf and her sister, the artist Vanessa Bell (1879-1961). Among the group's best known members were the art critic Clive Bell (Vanessa's husband), writer and social reformer Leonard Woolf (Virginia's husband), the writers Lytton Strachey and E. M. Forster and the critic Roger Fry. The group not only shared the pleasures of discussion and the enjoyment of beautiful objects, but they objected to the rigid conventions of Victorian England. The Bloomsbury Group had great influence on the arts in Great Britain. ■

English artists at this time studied in England, worked there and had little to do with French or German painting. Following the opening of the railroad, the town of St. Ives, Cornwall, in the far southwest of England, became filled with tourists and artists in the 1880s. St. Ives attracted landscape painters while the nearby town of Newlyn attracted figure painters. The artist Stanhope Forbes (1857–1947) first went to St. Ives in 1884, but found he liked Newlyn better. By 1885, artists were flocking to that resort.

Finnish artist Helène Schjerfbeck (1862–1946) stayed in St. Ives in 1888 and returned again the following year. She had studied in Paris and her favorite themes were children and seated figures. Around this time, internationally known Swedish artist, Anders Zorn (1860–1920) arrived, bringing stature to the colony. He was a successful portrait painter in London.

By the 1890s, Newlyn was in decline as the original members left, but St. Ives continued to grow and to be a vital English art colony. Forbes opened an art school there to boost the colony, but it was not until the mid-twentieth century that it once more became a center for the avant-garde. The painter Ben Nicholson (1894–1982) and his wife, the sculptor, Barbara Hepworth (1903–75), along with Christopher Wood (1901–30) moved there at the outbreak of World War II and St. Ives continued to be a lively center during the 1950s and 1960s.

This view from a hill, View of St. Ives, *was painted in oil on canvas by Scandinavian artist Helène Schjerfbeck in 1887. She painted many views around the town and frequently visited the Cornish colony.* ▼

5 | New Ways of Seeing

Color Theories and Modern Art

French chemist Eugène Chevreul was the director of the department of dyeing at the Gobelins Tapestry Factory in Paris. His book on color theories, *The Principles of Harmony and Contrast of Colors*, and *Their Application to the Arts*, was published in 1839. He observed that colors placed in proximity, influence and modify one another. He wrote that any isolated color will appear to be surrounded by a faint aureole of its complementary color; for example, green will have a red reflection. The optical mixing is done by the eye. He also noted that complementary colors used in large areas intensify and when they are used in small areas they make neutral tones. These theories were a revelation to the Impressionists and Post-Impressionists. Delacroix, who formulated his own color theories, was familiar with the work of Chevreul. Pissarro, Monet and Seurat had all read his book and applied the ideas in their work.

Pissarro and Seurat also studied the work of physicists Hermann Helmholtz, James Clerk Maxwell and Ogden N. Rood. In their work these scientists concluded that the observer's eye reconstructs the form and color of what is being perceived from the *prismatic* colors which compose it. All these color theories led Seurat to create a structured organization of color in his paintings and helped him form his Divisionist technique best seen in works like his masterpiece, *A Sunday Afternoon on the Island of la Grande Jatte*, 1884–86. ■

▲ *Georges Seurat's oil on canvas* Les Poseuses (The Models), *1888 shows the artist's model in three poses. His masterpiece* A Sunday Afternoon on the Island of la Grande Jatte, *painted between 1884 and 1886, appears in the painting on the left wall. The figures are locked into a rigid system of colored dots called Divisionism. The eye fuses the dots together to form larger areas of color.*

The Impressionists' spontaneous and loose painting style was challenged by a more scientific approach in the work of the Post-Impressionists who were experimenting with Pointillism and Divisionist techniques. Pointillism used dabs of color set on a white ground, while Divisionism used dabs of color set closely together so that the eye could fuse them together to form larger areas of colors. They did not use black but created it in their paintings through a subtle blend of dark colors.

The Post-Impressionist painter, Georges Seurat (1859–91) made his paintings by placing small dots of color side by side and letting the eye mix them together to produce rich, luminous colors. His was an intellectual art and one where the process was as important as the subject matter. He worked closely with painter Paul Signac (1863–1935). They experimented with optical theories and applied them to their work.

Color creates the structure of Seurat's paintings whereas the

24

The Eiffel Tower: A Symbol of Modernity

The Universal Exposition in Paris in 1889 was an exhibition staged to show the scientific and engineering achievements of France and Europe at the end of the nineteenth century. A Palace of Machines was planned to exhibit modern machinery.

The crowning achievement of French technology was the magnificent Eiffel Tower. Architectural engineers, Gustave Eiffel (1832–1923) and Victor Contomin, were commissioned to build the iron tower in 1887. It was completed on March 28, 1889, a month before the exposition opened and it was an instant sensation. The Eiffel Tower could be seen from every vantage point in Paris as it rose majestically up into the sky. It was the perfect modern symbol. ■

The great iron structure, the Eiffel Tower, *was built in 1889 for the Universal Exposition* ▶ *in Paris. It was a symbol for modernity and is now a landmark and an icon for the city of Paris.*

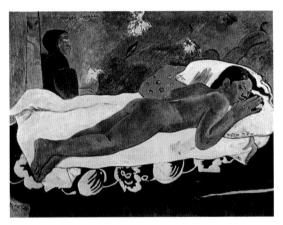

▲ *In* Spirit of the Dead Watching, *1892, painted in oil on burlap, Paul Gauguin combines the myths of the South Seas people with a Symbolist painting style.*

◀ *Odilon Redon's imagery in* The Cyclops, *1898, painted in oil on canvas, reveals an imaginative inner mind.*

Impressionists used color to show how scenes were always changing. Seurat's work is carefully calculated and highly organized. Seurat exhibited with the Impressionists in their last exhibition in 1886.

Another Post-Impressionist art movement called Symbolism developed around 1885. It was a movement of the visual arts and literature and was directly opposed to a scientific approach to art. Symbolism was an art of the inner mind. Symbolist artists were not interested in realism and recording the real world. They painted and wrote about things from their imaginations and used symbols to communicate their ideas to others. It was, in part a reaction throughout Europe to widespread political corruption and unrest. Artists questioned the world they lived in and looked inward for answers. The imagination and emotions began to be explored in art for inspiration, and perhaps even for some answers to the problems in the world.

The center of Symbolist activity was at the Cafe Volpini in Paris where Gauguin and the School of Pont-Aven artists exhibited in 1889. Gauguin, Émile Bernard and the others created dreamlike images with luxurious, decorative forms, that were full of symbolism. Gauguin brought many ideas together to form his complex paintings. He was not painting simple scenes but layered his work with different spiritual and mythical meanings drawn from different cultures and artistic styles. He retreated to Tahiti to rid himself of the decadence of European society. Tahiti offered a sense of spirituality and purity in the myths of the natives and their lifestyle. He drew on these things and created paintings that were imaginative and rooted in the native symbolism he found in Tahiti.

Odilon Redon's (1840–1916) work explores myths and portrays imaginary images. His paintings have a dreamy quality. Redon's work influenced Gauguin, particularly through his reliance on inner

25

▲ *Edvard Munch's expressive oil on canvas,*
Puberty, 1894, is a terrifying portrait of a
young girl on the verge of maturity.

Symbolist Poets

Symbolism began as a literary movement in the late nineteenth century. Suggestions of ideas were emphasized as opposed to direct descriptions. Images and feelings from the inner world of the artist played an important role in the works of these writers. Symbolist poets explored the musical properties of language in their poetry. Stéphane Mallarmé (1842–98) was the leading poet of the movement. In "Dice Thrown Never will Annul Chance," 1897, he experimented with the shapes the words made on the page like a musical score. He was fascinated by the mystery of language and stated, "the pleasure of discovering things little by little; suggestion, that is the dream."

Mallarmé and the poets Arthur Rimbaud and Paul Verlaine and others, wrote Symbolist poetry that was a reaction against Realism and the external world. It focused on the inner world of feeling and expression. ■

One of the greatest modern painters is Vincent
van Gogh. In The Night Cafe, *1888, through*
the aggressive color and movement of the
composition the artist explores the effect of the
light from a hanging lamp radiating around the
small cafe. ▼

thought and soft, curving form. Redon's reputation was established in Belgium and Holland where his spiritual art was better understood. A special retrospective of Redon's work was brought together in the 1903 Salon d'Automne in Paris. As a result his reputation grew.

In England, William Blake was a visionary artist who created a symbolic world in his paintings and writings. The figures in his works are classical in form and inhabit a fantasy world. Blake (1757–1827) had great influence on the Pre-Raphaelites. In turn, Edward Burne-Jones, one of the Pre-Raphaelites, had a strong influence on French Symbolism and he is considered one of the major painters of the late nineteenth century in Europe. The artist James Ensor (1860–1949), another Symbolist, working in Belgium used masks, exotic toys and other curiosities in his paintings to suggest connections with what was going on in the artist's mind. His work influenced the Surrealists. Edvard Munch (1863–1944) in Norway created works also inspired by Symbolism. His later works were powerful statements of feeling and emotion. Munch's subject matter is melancholy and suggests deeper meanings beyond the surface. He was influenced by the intense emotion presented through simplified blocks of pure color in Gauguin's paintings. The young Picasso, in his Blue and Rose periods, came under the influence of Symbolism.

Some Symbolist ideas are also seen in the work of Dutch painter Vincent van Gogh. Van Gogh's paintings are filled with emotion expressed through his strong brushwork.

In photography, the work of Englishman Frederick Evans (1853–1943) shows Symbolist influences. In his photograph, *On*

▲ *Frederick Evans, influenced by Symbolism,* *photographed* On Sussex Downs *about 1900.*

Sussex Downs, the curved lines of the landscape create a dreamscape with a meandering road. The sparse landscape is other worldly. Evans never altered his negatives and took pride in creating truthful scenes of nature.

Eugène Atget (1857–1927) in France, recorded images of things he saw in the city streets of Paris in his photographs. He did not try to manipulate the viewer but simply recorded what was there before him. His photographs, however, suggest there are deeper meanings to his images of the real world.

Leon Bakst designed the costumes and set for Diaghilev's 1912 ballet, The Afternoon of a Faun. ▼

World of Art Group __

The members of the World of Art Group, under the leadership of Alexander Benois (1870–1960) were the leaders of the avant-garde art movement in Russia in the 1890s. Sergei Diaghilev and Léon Bakst were also members. The group was heavily influenced by the Symbolists. They joined together in St. Petersburg in 1898 to restore the culture they felt had been lost in Russia. They wanted to create a Russian international center for the arts and they hoped to establish a serious exchange of ideas with the larger European community. ■

▲ *Cropping and close-up views gave deeper meaning to Eugène Atget's subjects as in* Fontaine de la Tête du Boeuf, *1903.*

Ballet Russe de Monte Carlo_____

Sergei Diaghilev, a founding member of the World of Art group in the 1890s in Russia, had widespread interests and he was able to bring together a diverse group of artists, musicians and dancers to collaborate in his ground-breaking theatrical presentations. He created the *Ballet Russe de Monte Carlo* which produced dancers like Leonid Massine, Anna Pavlova and Vassily Nijinsky. The composer Igor Stravinsky (1882–1971) worked with him, creating important music for ballets. Stravinsky's *Rite of Spring* was choreographed by Nijinsky. When it opened in Paris in 1913, it caused a riot.

Through his contacts in Paris, Diaghilev got Picasso, Bakst, Léger, Chagall and many other artists to create costumes and sets for the company. He brought ballet into the modern age with his avant-garde productions. He left behind a magnificent tradition of dance and a sense of artistic collaboration that carries through to the present. ■

6 Cézanne, the Father of Modern Painting

In The Bay from L'Estaque, *painted in oil* ▶
on canvas about 1885, Paul Cézanne began to
reduce the houses to basic forms.

Paving the Way_____

Pablo Picasso and Georges Braque (1882–1963) admired Cézanne's work and Braque went to L'Estaque in the south of France to paint the landscape that had occupied Cézanne. Taking the same view of the houses there, Braque filled the canvas with blocks of form that he pushed to the surface, further breaking-up the space. The work created a sense of deep space without using perspective, a concept begun by Cézanne and fully realized by the Cubists, of whom Picasso and Braque are the best known. ■

Paul Cézanne broke forms into planes of color
in Boy in a Red Vest, *1890–95, painted in oil*
on canvas. ▼

One of the most influential artists of the modern era was Paul Cézanne (1839–1906) whose innovative way of breaking up space and simplifying objects into their basic forms led directly to Modernism in the twentieth century. His simplification of objects into spheres, cones and cylinders paved the way for Cubism and then for abstraction.

Cézanne was born in Aix-en-Provence in the South of France, into a wealthy family of merchants. He attended law school in 1859 and his path as a traditional upper class man seemed assured. But, the young Cézanne was intensely interested in art and enrolled in a course at the School of Design in Aix. He went to Paris in 1861 and studied at the Académie Suisse. He frequented the galleries of the Louvre, and made the acquaintance of the painter Armand Guillaumin (1841–1927) and the young writer, Emile Zola.

Cézanne returned to Aix and worked in his father's bank. He continued painting, producing a number of portraits and decorating the walls of the Joseph de Boffan estate that his parents bought in 1859. By 1862, the artist returned to Paris determined to become a serious painter. He made friends with some of the Impressionists painters, but preferred the work of Courbet and Delacroix, who wanted to paint "with guts" as did Cézanne.

Cézanne's early paintings were made with thick paint that he applied with a palette knife. This gave way in 1867 to paintings that

▲ *In* Still Life with Basket of Apples, *1890–94, which was painted in oil on canvas, Paul Cézanne simplified the forms and used areas of colors to model the form.*

The Dreyfus Case

In 1894, a sensational trial was held in France accusing a French army captain of treason. The young officer, Alfred Dreyfus (1859–1935), a Jew, was arrested, tried and imprisoned for life. The Dreyfus case tore the country apart as accusations of antisemitism were hurled at the army and the government. The press wrote thinly veiled antisemitic stories accusing Dreyfus of the crime. There were fist fights in cafes as Parisians chose sides.

In 1896, evidence showing that the real criminal was a Major Esterhazy came to light. Neither the military nor the government could admit to charges of forgery, intimidation and bias against a Jewish officer. They campaigned against a retrial and Dreyfus remained in prison.

In 1899, Dreyfus was finally pardoned, but not until 1906 was the verdict overturned and Dreyfus released. ∎

This oil on canvas of Mont Sainte-Victoire, ▶ *1904-06, is part of the landscape near Cézanne's home in Aix. Cézanne broke up the space into small facets of color and form.*

used bold brushwork. In 1870, he went to L'Estaque to paint and to avoid the military draft. A year later when the Franco-Prussian War ended, he returned to Paris. The following year he went to live in Auvers-sur-Oise, where he worked with Guillaumin and Pissarro for two years. Under Pissarro, Cézanne learned to use smaller brushstrokes and to build up form slowly and more intricately.

In 1876, his mature artistic style emerged and his painting began to deal with issues of light, volume and structure. After the 1877 Impressionist exhibition, he chose a life of solitude in Aix. Only his work remained important. He painted landscapes, portraits and still lifes.

Living in Aix, away from the influences of Impressionist and Post-Impressionist experiments, Cézanne set about analyzing the underlying structure of the images he painted. He developed his own visual language. He broke with conventional perspective and, instead, created depth through layered planes, shifting and recreating space in his paintings. Using color he created forms that looked self-sufficient and powerful. He simplified and discarded irrelevant details.

Structure is the most important element in Cézanne's painting and this developed to maturity around 1900. Objects became sculptural forms. He created light and dark areas by placing one color next to another. His last works, scenes of Mont Sainte-Victoire, executed from 1904 to 1906, are Cézanne's most radical in construction. While still making a recognizable and beautiful landscape, he fashioned pictures where each brushstroke existed fully on its own, but also formed an integral part of the composition. Cézanne analyzed each shape and form and reduced them to their basic components. He revolutionized modern painting.

Color is Liberated

▲ *Color is the most important element in Matisse's oil on canvas,* The Blue Window *of 1911. It constructs the space in this work.*

Matisse's Cut-outs

For the last decade of his life, Matisse was in poor health and it was difficult for him to paint. Aided by his studio assistants, the ailing artist directed the creation of work from his wheelchair or from his bed. Using prepainted paper prepared under his direction, Matisse cut out shapes and with a long stick pointed to the spot on the canvas where they were to be glued. His determination to continue working was remarkable. He produced some of his finest work during these last years. ■

The first artistic revolution of the twentieth century was the liberation of color. A group called the *Fauves,* whose name means wild beasts, were led by Henri Matisse (1869–1954). Their canvases exploded with energy and pure color. They would paint the sky orange, the trees red or whatever their rich imaginations envisioned. The surfaces of their paintings were covered with bright hues using no shading. Their eccentric use of color created dimension without modeling. These canvases were exciting, unpredictable and definitely new. They used color to express their inner feelings.

The work of Matisse and the *Fauves* outraged the public when it was shown at the Salon d'Automne, 1905, in Paris. No one had seen color used in this way before. Their experiments began in 1899 when Albert Marquet (1875–1947) worked with Matisse. A few years later they were joined by André Derain (1880–1954) and Maurice de Vlaminck (1876–1958). Derain and Matisse made the first *Fauve* paintings at Collioure, near Paris.

In Germany, the German Expressionist group *Die Brücke* (The Bridge) was formed in 1905 in Dresden. Fritz Bleyl (1880–1966) founded the group that included Ernst Ludwig Kirchner, Erich Heckel and Karl Schmitt-Rottluff. They hoped their work would form a bridge to art of the future. They used color in their work to express emotion. The formation of the group marked the beginning of modern art in Germany.

From 1905, they exhibited together regularly. They were trying to incorporate all the new ideas being explored in Europe at the time into their own work. They had frequent meetings in Kirchner's studio and they shared an interest in tribal art. The group broke up in 1913 but Expressionism continued to be a relevant style for German artists throughout the century.

By 1909, Munich was the center of German art activity where the

◀ *In 1943, Henri Matisse began a project called* Jazz. *The* Cowboy, 1947, *made from colored, paper cut-outs, is one of the pieces made for this project.*

▲ *The expressive* Market Place with Red Tower, *1915, was painted in oil on canvas by the German Expressionist Ernst Ludwig Kirchner. It shows the influence of Fauvism and Cubism in its dramatic movement and color.*

Vassily Kandinsky is credited with creating the first abstract painting in 1910. The First Abstract Watercolor *is an abstraction of great power, but the remains of figures, animals and the landscape used as a starting point for the work can still be seen.* ▼

▲ *The large blue animals in* Der Blue Horses, *1911, by* Der Blaue Reiter *co-founder Franz Marc, move like dream creatures in a landscape.*

New Artists' Federation of Munich was formed. The group included artists Wassily Kandinsky, Franz Marc, Alexej von Jawlensky, Gabriele Münter and Alfred Kubin. Their first exhibition was held at the Gallery Tannhauser in Munich in December 1909. Their aim was to unite all the new artistic movements and to bring a spiritual element to them. They renamed their group, *Der Blaue Reiter* (The Blue Rider). It became one of the most important movements in modern art. They used elements from Russian folk art, with its lively color and loose composition, in their work. Their forms, line and color became progressively more abstract.

Franz Marc (1880–1916), whose lively paintings of blue horses and dream creatures, said that they wanted, "to create a tradition; not just live off one." The outbreak of World War I dispersed the group.

The Fauves, *Die Brücke* and *Der Blaue Reiter* revolutionized art at the dawn of the twentieth century. Through their work, the door was opened so that modern artists could use color in a new way and express their ideas with freedom.

Folk Art Influences

The seventeenth-century Russian folk artist Vasilii Koran made woodcuts of the Last Judgment. He used folk images with floating angels, flattened perspective and magical ideas. These images were used by Kandinsky in his early abstract work. The trumpets seen in the folk images are used over and over again in Kandinsky's paintings from 1910 to 1913. Religious themes and old Russian folk tales interested Kandinsky and he freely worked them into his art. ■

8 The Break-up of Form

A Prolific Artist

Pablo Picasso's early work, influenced by Impressionism, gave way to figurative painting. In his Blue Period, 1901 to 1904, Picasso painted elongated figures in shades of blue. In the Rose Period, 1904–06, he painted harlequins and circus performers in soft hues of red. Picasso's Cubist ideas formulated in 1907 never left his work. Although he always strived to find a new way to express himself, Picasso's portraits, images of minotaurs and bullfighters and his prints and sculpture continued to refer to Cubism. ■

▲ *One of the great paintings of twentieth century art is Pablo Picasso's oil on canvas* Demoiselles d'Avignon, 1907. *It marked the beginning of Cubism with its new way of breaking up space.*

One of the most important developments in art took place when Georges Braque (1882–1963) met Pablo Picasso in 1907. Braque and Picasso shared a deep respect for the work of Paul Cézanne and were enthusiastic about tribal art which they both collected and displayed on the walls of their studios. They embarked on a unique collaboration of exploration and experimentation. Their daily visits to each other's studios produced a spirited exchange of ideas and a body of exciting work which led to the founding of Cubism in 1908.

Picasso took the first step toward Cubism. He worked on his painting *Les Demoiselles d'Avignon* in great secrecy. When he had finished it in 1907, he invited a number of artists and critics to see it. They were shocked by what they saw. Matisse became angry, Braque was stunned and the critic Guillaume Apollinaire was very negative in his criticism. The painting was aggressive and direct, combining refer-

▲ Houses at L'Estaque, *painted in oil on canvas 1908, by Georges Braque, explores Cézanne's ideas about space and form which led to Cubism.*

Cubism Survives

When World War I began in August 1914, the association of Braque and Picasso came to an end. Braque joined the army and Picasso remained in France working. After the war, Cubism became a symbol of the destruction of Europe due to the war. Just as Cubists artists broke up or destroyed objects and space in their paintings, the war had destroyed Europe. Despite the negative associations Cubism survived the war. Picasso referred to it often in his work and Braque continued to make colorful Cubist paintings. Cubism continues to have a major influence today. ■

▲ Accordionist, *painted in oil on canvas by Pablo Picasso, 1911, is an example of Analytic Cubism. The figure of the musician is fragmented almost to the point of abstraction.*

ences to ancient Iberian sculpture and African masks. The response kept Picasso from showing the work for many years. It is today one of the great paintings of twentieth century art.

Georges Braque began experimenting with elements of Cubist space in his work after meeting Picasso. He painted *The Large Nude* in 1907 which showed the change from Fauvism to a new concern for structure. He began to break up space in his paintings like Cézanne, and reduce objects to the basic geometric forms of the cone, cylinder and cube. Braque produced a group of paintings, including, *Houses at L'Estaque*, 1908, using the same landscape and viewpoint that Cézanne had painted successfully a number of years earlier. The architecture and the surrounding landscape of the painting interconnect and interlock and are more abstract than Cézanne's approach.

The German art dealer Daniel-Henry Kahnweiler gave Braque a show in Paris, the first Cubist exhibition ever held. The Kahnweiler Gallery became the home of Cubism. At the same time Pablo Picasso had begun to work in a similar way using Cézanne's idea of simplified planes. Treating the figure and background equally, Braque and Picasso reduced objects in their paintings to their basic forms. The period between 1907 and 1909 is considered the first phase of Cubism when both artists were firmly under Cézanne's influence.

Continued experiments led the two artists to the second Cubist phase, called Analytic Cubism, which lasted from 1910 to 1912. In Analytic Cubism, the object was fragmented and displayed from several angles at once. Renaissance perspective was rejected and the traditional means of representing reality were abandoned. Each object and the ground was shattered into small cubes, like an image seen in a broken mirror. The many facets of the object were shown from multiple points of view. Paintings became almost abstract with only small elements remaining recognizable. The limited use of color in Analytic Cubism helped to emphasize the structure. Picasso's *Ma Jolie* and Braque's *The Portuguese*, both painted in 1911, show this phase of Cubism at its best and most inventive.

Picasso and Braque also introduced fragments of words into their paintings and images. Paper, textiles, wood and string were also glued to a surface. These works which combine paint and other objects are called collages. Picasso created the first collage in 1912, entitled *Still Life With Chair Caning*, by taking rope, a piece of oilcloth with a picture of chair caning on it and paint. This new phase was called Synthetic Cubism. In Synthetic Cubism artists reconstructed the space and objects of their works with fragmented forms. They built these elements with found objects and fragments of type. Color was reintroduced into their work of this period. The forms in this work are large, flat, shapes of color.

◄ Fernand Léger used the mechanical forms of the modern world in his Cubist paintings. In The City, 1919, *painted in oil on canvas, the sculptural treatment of pipes and street signs gives a monumental and abstract feeling to the work. Léger found beauty in the machinery and mass-produced objects of the industrialized, modern world. During World War II Léger left Nazi-controlled Europe to live in the United States where he taught at Mills College in California and Yale University. When he returned to France in 1945 his style remained unchanged but the themes of his paintings became political and expressed an interest in the working class.*

Fernand Léger (1881–1955) and Juan Gris (1887–1927) were also Cubists. Léger simplified forms in his paintings so they seem monumental. He used primary colors and black, white and gray. He celebrated the machine age with its polished surfaces and intricate pipes and machinery in his work so that even his figures look like machines. In *The City*, he painted the modern urban architecture of a technological society. Gris's work was in keeping with Picasso's and Braque's, but more rhythmic and solid. Gris often added sand to his paint to create texture and richer color. He started with the basic form and built up the object from it. "Cézanne turns a bottle into a cylinder, but I make a bottle—a particular bottle—out of a cylinder," Gris explained.

World War I broke up the collaboration between Braque and Picasso and Cubism came under attack. The violent break-up of space and form which was the hallmark of Cubist painting was equated to the destruction of Europe during World War I. Many artists returned to Classicism, an art that looked to the glory of the past and was better understood by the general public. However, the Cubist movement that Picasso and Braque had founded revolutionized art in the twentieth century and continues to influence artists to this day.

The invention of the airplane in the early years of the twentieth century changed history and man's relationship with the world. With the first powered flight in 1903 by the American Wright brothers and the flight over the English Channel by French aviator Louis Bleriot two years later, a new interest in speed, motion and aerial perspective among artists developed. The Futurist movement that rose up in Italy in 1909 was the first art movement of the twentieth century that tried

Rise of Futurism

Futurism developed in reaction to Italy's slowness to develop technologically in the early 1900s. The Futurists felt that Italy fell far behind other countries in terms of modern progress. Old cultural systems were rejected and new, modern ideas were embraced fully by the Futurists. Even the destruction of museums and libraries, temples of the old ways, was considered. Speed, new ideas and violent warfare to cleanse the country of its old ways and to prepare it for modernism, were glorified. Futurists philosophically backed the outbreak of World War I in 1914 but the movement began to die as followers did in the war. However, in 1922 when the Fascist leader Benito Mussolini (1883–1945) came to power, the ideas of the Futurists were resurrected to help the dictator in his attempt to make Italy a world power. ■

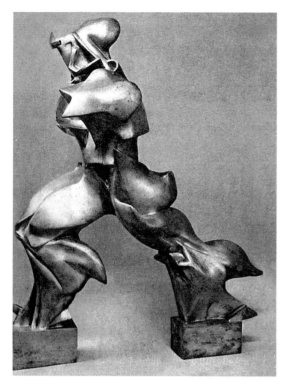

▲ *The Futurists were interested in movement and speed. Umberto Boccioni was a painter and a sculptor. In his bronze sculpture,* Unique Forms of Continuity in Space, *1913, he used lines of force to create this figure in motion.*

Motion was the concern of the Futurist artist Giacomo Balla in his oil on canvas, Dynamism of a Dog on A Leash (Leash in Motion), *1912. The dog's feet are painted to show the rapid sequence of movements as it walks along the street.* ▼

to change society through art. The Futurists not only glorified modern technology, but were especially interested in the idea of speed. Science and anything new were important to Futurist artists. They hated the past and academic ideas about art and glorified the modern world. Progress, speed and change were the main themes of Futurist art which were tied into social concerns in Italy as that country began to modernize after World War I.

The main artists of the Futurist movement were Umberto Boccioni, Carlo Carra, Giacomo Balla and Gino Severini. They were influenced by Cubism, X-ray photography and the sequenced photographs of Eadweard Muybridge (1830–1904) which showed the flow of movements of human figures and animals.

An artistic revolution in Russia was connected to the social uprisings political turmoil, and riots there in the early years of the twentieth century which set the stage for the successful 1917 revolution. Cubism and Futurism influenced the Russian avant-garde. After visiting Picasso, Russian artist Vladimir Tatlin (1885–1953), became the leader of an art movement he called Constructivism. He founded it in 1913. Its members rejected easel painting in favor of an abstract, geometric style of art that often was constructed from industrial materials such as glass and plastic. Tatlin was joined by the artists Naum Gabo, Antoine Pevsner and Alexander Rodchenko. Another avant-garde art movement, called Suprematism, was launched in opposition to Constructivism. The founder of the Suprematist movement was Kazimir Malevich (1878–1935) who, like the Constructivists, was influenced by Cubism and Futurism. Suprematists called their early work Cubo-Futurism. Malevich produced paintings that generally were made up of basic geometric shapes and a limited range of colors.

His art was radically abstract and stressed the spiritual. He wanted to reduce art to nothing and then rebuild from the bottom to produce an art with a "supremacy of pure feeling and perception."

The Constructivists and the Suprematists both believed that their art could be used as a tool for revolution in Russia. Each group felt

Vorticism

Futurism had a great influence on an English art movement called Vorticism. Started before World War I, its main followers were the painters Wyndham Lewis, C.R.W. Nevinson, William Roberts, Edward Wadsworth and sculptors Jacob Epstein and Henri Gaudier-Brzeska. The Vorticists used harsh Futurist angles and diagonals in their work. This was the first organized move to make abstract art in England. ■

that through art a universal sign system could be created and understood by everyone. Each wanted to create change in life through their art.

Russian avant-garde artists felt their advanced aesthetic ideas could be used in the service of a new Russia. El Lissitzky (1890–1941), one of the followers of Malevich, designed architecture presenting ideas for ultra-modern buildings. Many of the artists created art for kiosks, which are small stands where leaflets and posters were handed out. Posters made by artists like Gustav Klutsis (1895–1944) were strong political statements about the new social order in Russia. Many were produced using an innovative

Kazimir Malevich reduced painting to pure geometry to create a universal language for the new, modern Russia. In Black Square and Red Square, *painted in oil on canvas about 1913, he created a totally abstract painting.* ▼

▲ *Vladimir Tatlin, the leader of the avant-garde in Russia, visited Picasso in 1913, an experience that changed the way he worked. Tatlin's painting called* Model *shows Picasso's Cubist influence. The same year, he founded the Constructivist movement.*

War and Revolution

Tsar Nicholas II (1868–1918) of Russia came to power in 1894. Crop failures and industrial crises led to unrest throughout the country. After Russia's defeat by Japan in 1905, cries for change became aggressive. Riots in 1905, killed hundreds of demonstrators and set the stage for revolution.

Nicholas II was forced to abdicate in March 1917 and a provisional government was formed. In October 1917, Vladimir Lenin (1870–1924) and Leon Trotsky (1879–1940) came to power when the provisional government was overthrown. In July 1918 the Tsar and his Royal family were executed. Lenin died in 1924, Joseph Stalin (1879–1953) took control and, by 1926, Trotsky was being forced out. A reign of terror began as thousands were killed to ensure Stalin's control.

The October Revolution of 1917 was intended to form a classless society, a Marxist state where all would be equal and united. Artists rallied to the cause and produced exciting, revolutionary art. Reform and modernization were aided by their active participation. This all came to a halt when Stalin took office. The use of art as a tool for building a new society gave way to a conformist vision of art as propaganda when Stalin restricted the kind of art acceptable to the Russian state. ■

Victory Over the Sun

The Futurist opera, *Victory Over the Sun*, was performed in St. Petersburg, Russia, in 1913. The painter Kazimir Malevich designed the sets and costumes, Alexei Kruchenykh wrote the libretto, the poet Velimir Klebnikov wrote the prologue and Mikhail Matyushin composed the music. The opera was very avant-garde and even a new language called Zaum was used to create a sense of freedom and exploration. The artists were influenced by the writings of Russian philosopher P.D. Ouspensky (1878–1947) who said, "All art is just one entire illogicality." This sense of the illogical was demonstrated in the wild costumes, abstract sets and the fragments of words, sentences and sounds used to create the opera. Through a series of backdrops and Cubist-inspired designs for costumes coupled with the illogical language and music, The artists hoped to achieve a higher understanding of art and life. ■

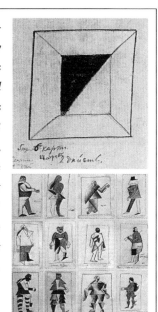

These ▶ drawings show Malevich's backcloth and costume designs for the 1913 Futurist opera, Victory Over the Sun. *The abstract backcloth (above) was similar to early Suprematist paintings.*

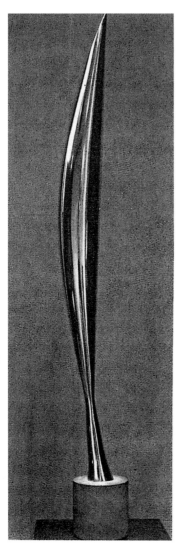

Constantin ▶ Brancusi was one of the great sculptors of the twentieth century. He polished the brass sculpture, Bird in Space, *approx. 1927, to a high degree to achieve a reflective surface. The stylized shape makes the bird form appear to move upward as if the bird was in flight.*

and creative style of photomontage. Photographs and words were combined in new ways to present ideas and messages. Theater productions and visionary architectural projects were all created with the new Russia as inspiration

In the late 1920s, the government became more restrictive and the free expression of artists' ideas was seen as dangerous to the Communist regime. Abstraction was forbidden. The government called on all artists to make Social Realist art that would document the struggle of workers in the new society. This was a call to old ways, where art was controlled. Surprisingly, most of the artists complied. They stopped experimenting with abstraction and tried to find a style that would conform to government-sanctioned standards.

The sculpture of Romanian artist Constantin Brancusi (1876–1957) marked the development of another new art form. Influenced by the work of Rodin, Gauguin and primitive carvings, Brancusi reduced natural forms to abstract simplicity. The result was a sculpture of unique purity of form. He rejected modeling and carved directly in marble or limestone. He combined wood, marble and bronze in some of his work, blending the different textures. He often polished the surface of his bronze work until it gleamed. The sleek form and polished surface of *Bird in Space* shows how Brancusi simplified his subject. The bird seems to rise up in flight before the viewer's eyes.

Cubism, Futurism, Constructivism and Suprematism set a standard for abstraction in the beginning of the century. These movements provided a framework on which artists could build their concepts and ideas for many generations.

9 Chance and the Unconscious

▲ *Jean Arp's* Mountain, Table, Anchors, Navel, *1925, is made of cut-outs glued where they fell.*

Kurt Schwitter's collage, Aerated VIII *of 1942, is the kind of work he called a* Merz *picture.* ▼

On June 28, 1914, Archduke Ferdinand of Austria was assassinated in Sarajevo, Yugoslavia. A month later, World War I erupted in Europe. This war caused devastation throughout Europe with over 13 million deaths before its end in 1918. Artist, Jean Arp (1887–1966) said, "Repelled by the slaughterhouse of the World War, we turned to art. We searched for an elementary art that would, we thought, save mankind from the furious madness of these times...."

Arp, along with the poet Tristan Tzara, writers Richard Hulsenbeck and Hugo Ball, and painter Sophie Taeuber-Arp met at the Cabaret Voltaire, in Zurich, Switzerland in February 1916, and founded Dada. It had been said they stuck a pin in a French dictionary and hit on the word for hobbyhorse, *dada*. The Dadaists relied on the element of chance in their work so this was a perfect way to find a name for the group. Tzara wrote a manifesto and the movement was launched.

By 1917 Dada emerged in New York and in Berlin, Cologne and Hanover in Germany. The Dadaists attacked the establishment. They believed that reason and logic had led to the war, so anarchy and the irrational would lead to salvation. Their art would not be controlled by reason but would rely on chance.

Marcel Duchamp_____

By taking an ordinary object and presenting it as a work of art Marcel Duchamp made his first ready-made in 1913. He broke all the rules for high art. Duchamp took a bicycle wheel and a wooden stool, placed the wheel on top of the stool and called it art. They were now a piece of sculpture because the artist said so. This was a radical thing to do in the early part of the twentieth century. Duchamp's innovation, inventiveness and intellect had a tremendous impact on art in the latter part of the century and his influence continues today. ■

This is Marcel Duchamp's infamous ▶ *entry for the Independents Exhibition of 1917. The Fountain by R. Mutt was made from a porcelain urinal turned upside down.*

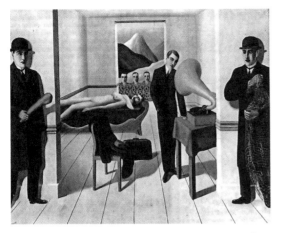

▲ *In* The Menaced Assassins, *1926, painted in oil on canvas, René Magritte showed a murder scene. One assassin listens to a phonograph while others lurk behind doors or lean out of windows making a dreamlike scene.*

Freud and the "Unconscious"

Sigmund Freud's techniques of free-association of ideas and dream interpretation, developed as a method of treatment for mental disorders, probed the inner recesses of the mind for clues to behavior. These were techniques exciting to the Surrealist artists looking for a way to tap the subconscious for ideas and to reveal their innermost feelings. ■

Woman With Her Throat Cut, *1932, by Alberto Giacometti shows the sculptor's Surrealist beginnings. The abstract, bronze figure takes on a menacing look with its jagged edges.* ▼

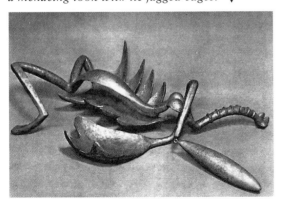

Chance played a crucial role in Dada, especially in the work of Arp and Duchamp. Arp cut out shapes and dropped them onto a board. He glued the pieces where they fell. Marcel Duchamp (1887–1978) used accidents in his work. When his masterpiece, *The Bride Stripped Bare By Her Bachelors, Even*, was cracked in transport, he decided that this was chance and felt that now the work was complete.

When Surrealism began to emerge in 1922 many Dada artists made the transition to this new movement associated with the theories of the psychoanalyst Sigmund Freud (1856–1939). They were aware of his writings such as *The Interpretation of Dreams*, in which he probed the unconscious for the meaning of dreams. The Surrealists began making drawings using automatic writing in which they let their minds direct their hands. In their paintings they recreated eerie landscapes of the mind where familiar objects and people were placed in odd juxtapositions and in strange contexts. A new reality, one of the inner mind, was formed in the work of Max Ernst, Joan Miró and

Salvador Dali used a super-realistic painting style to heighten the dreamscape he created in Invention of the Monsters, *1937, painted in oil on canvas.* ▼

the Belgian, René Magritte. In 1929, Salvador Dali (1904–1989) joined the movement. Dali's films and paintings embrace the Surrealist spirit.

The impact of Surrealism on other art movements was profound. The work of Joan Miró (1893–1983) and the sculptor Alberto Giacometti (1901–1966) used Surrealist ideas. Giorgio de Chirico (1888–1978) called his art metaphysical painting. His figures, seen in desolate landscapes with large shadows, create an eerie scene. These works are close in feeling to Surrealism but use its vocabulary in a different way.

10 Between the Wars

Käthe Kollwitz

German artist Käthe Kollwitz (1867–1945) used social protest in her art producing powerful black and white etchings and lithographs of human suffering. Her compassion for the poor and interest in better conditions for workers led her to create works of art showing their plight. She was influenced by the work of Edvard Munch, Honore Daumier and Vincent van Gogh. Kollwitz was married to a doctor whose practice was limited to the poor.

She is also known for her prints and sculptures on the theme of mother and child. Her work was aways a personal statement and protest against the suffering of the poor. ■

▲ *Käthe Kollwitz's lithograph,* Death Seizing a Woman, *1934, is a powerful expressionistic work calling for much needed social reform.*

▲ *George Grosz's drawing* The Mad on The Rampage, *1915–16, shows the madness of the war years in Germany.*

Between the two world wars, Germany went through extreme social and political changes. Its defeat in 1918 created a climate of disillusion and despair. A struggle took place between far-left and far-right political factions resulting in a Social Democrat Revolution in November 1918. Artists responded to the times of revolution. Berlin Dada became overtly political.

Some German artists used photomontage, a collage made with photographic images, to make their political points. Photomontage was said to have been invented in Berlin by George Grosz (1893–1959) and John Heartfield (1891–1968) in 1916. This claim was disputed by Raoul Hausmann ((1886–1971) and Hannah Höch

(1889–1979) who said that they had the idea first. These four artists used photomontage to its full potential, creating an art of social and political significance. They used words and images pulled from magazines and books. Hausmann said that they were creating a "new image of the chaos of an age of war and revolution."

In *Cut With A Cake Knife*, 1919, Höch ruptured the surface of her work with fragments of words and images to shock the viewer out of complacency. Her art reflected the chaos the war and revolution had brought to the country. In *Collage*, produced in 1920, Höch used body parts of different sizes put together for startling effect. Hausmann's work blended images with strongly political words.

By 1924, Germany was shifting more and more to the right politically and there was rapid inflation. A new cynicism gripped the country. The biting satire of George Grosz attacked the weak government and bourgeois society. His criticism of the ruling class was unforgiving and called for social reform. In 1925, Grosz became a member of the New Objectivity (*Neue Sachlichkeit*) movement. He, along with Otto Dix (1891–1969) and Max Beckmann, brought a new realism to their work. Dix used a meticulous realism and showed distorted figures from strange angles to address the issue of the horrors of war. In 1944, during World War II, Dix produced a book of engravings entitled *War* showing the inhumanity and devastation of war.

John Heartfield created the most provocative political art of the group. Through the use of photomontage and printed text, Heartfield aggressively attacked the rise of Adolf Hitler (1889–1945) and the Nazi Party in Germany in the 1930s. In *The Spirit of Geneva*, 1932, a dove is speared by a sword as a Nazi flag waves over a government building

▲ *Hannah Höch used images and words that referred to Germany and the very political Dadaists in her collage* Cut with A Cake Knife, *1919.*

◀ *John Heartfield's overtly political photomontages, such as* The Spirit of Geneva, *1932, were serious indictments of the rise of Hitler and the Nazis in the 1930s.*

41

▲ *Heartfield's* A Pan-German, 2 November 1933, *is a strong anti-Nazi statement.*

The Bauhaus

▲ *Paul Klee (1879–1940) taught at the Bauhaus and had a major influence on modern artists. In* Dance, Monster, To My Soft Song!, 1922, *Klee's beautiful linear elements create a world that is both childlike and sophisticated.*

A new type of art school was founded in Weimar, Germany, in 1919 by architect Walter Gropius (1883–1969). The school was called The Bauhaus and it merged fine art and craftmaking. Gropius hired a distinguished group of artists to teach at his school. He invited Wassily Kandinsky, Paul Klee, Oscar Schlemmer and Johannes Itten to create a curriculum giving the students a complete experience in the arts. These men wanted to take each discipline out of its isolation and explore all facets of art so that each Bauhaus student received a thorough art education. The students well-made crafts were sold throughout Europe and the school became a self-supporting institution. Through its communal art activities the Bauhaus could work for social progress. The Bauhaus was closed by the Nazis in 1933, but its influence continues to be felt. ∎

Wassily Kandinsky's late style became very geometric. Composition IX, No. 626, 1936, *has hard edge shapes and strong colors like work produced during the period he spent teaching at The Bauhaus.* ▼

in the background. The message, that peace is dead, is very clear. *A Pan-German*, 1933, uses a photograph of Julius Streicher, the leader of the Nazi paramilitary force placed on top of a police file photograph of a bloody murder victim. It is a direct statement indicting Streicher and the Nazis. Heartfield made hundreds of photomontages during this dangerous and decadent time. In 1930s Germany there was a complete breakdown of society. Corruption was rampant as the economy was failing and the nation turned towards Hitler's regime to save them. The worst was yet to come.

Photography was part of the curriculum at The Bauhaus art school in Weimar, Germany. Laszlo Moholy-Nagy (1895–1946), who taught there, was experimenting with various processes and styles of photography. Moholy-Nagy was part of the "New Photographers" group that believed photography was the universal language of the new, modern

▲ *Brassai photographed the darker side of Parisian life. His* Street Fair, *1933, shows a side-show barker at a carnival.*

Early European film __

In France, the motion picture was first taken seriously as an art form. On December 28, 1895, when the Lumière brothers showed the first film to the public projected on a screen, it was an instant success. In 1896, Georges Meliés, another Frenchman, began making films. He used elaborate sets and costumes to create special effects. Erich Pommer, the German filmmaker, also used sets and costumes in his films. In *The Cabinet of Dr. Caligari* of 1919, Pommer used strong black and white images and shadows and strange angles to mimic German Expressionist paintings. In the late 1920s, Hans Richter made Dada films and the Spaniards Louis Bunuel and Salvador Dali collaborated to make Surrealist films. The Soviets worked with film in its early days and contributed technically to raise the standards of the medium. ■

world. Moholy-Nagy's dedication to the medium led him to state, "The illiterate of the future will be the people who know nothing of photography rather than those who are ignorant of the art of writing."

In France, another group of photographers was documenting life in the city. André Kertész (1894–1985) came to Paris from Hungary in 1925. He took pictures of people on the streets and in cafes. He photographed Parisian billboards and buildings and his work had a great influence on French photography in general. He encouraged his friend, the painter Gyula Halasz (1899–1984), who changed his name to Brassai, to dedicate himself to photography.

Brassai filmed the underside of Parisian life and the city at night. His book, *Paris By Night*, 1933, contained sixty-two photographs showing cafes, working-class neighborhoods, carnivals and assorted odd characters of the great city. Like Kertész, he recorded the small events that revealed the true story of urban life. They each set a new standard for photo-journalism and their work was reproduced in magazines all over Europe. In the 1950s, Kertész produced a series of abstracted nudes which he called *Distortions*, which recall the sleek, organic sculpture of Brancusi.

During the period between the wars, motion pictures became an important medium for artistic expression. The films of Russian filmmaker Sergei Eisenstein (1898–1948) were innovative and explored the use of photomontage. His brilliant film, *Potemkin*, 1925, was the first instance of photomontage used in the movies. Telling the story of a mutiny by Russian sailors aboard the battleship *Potemkin* which was docked in the town of Odessa, Eisenstein used fast cutting and collage effects to create tension and conflict. As a Marxist, the filmmaker thought that this montage process would create a sequence of collisions that the viewer would experience and, through them, experience the conflict in society. In 1938, Eisenstein made the film *Alexander Nevsky* which tells the story of the Russian army fighting invading German knights in the Middle Ages. The great Russian composer Sergei Prokofief (1891–1953) composed the music. A fight scene on the ice shows small cracks beginning to form as horses move across a frozen river. The music matches the visual action perfectly and heightens the experience.

Eisenstein's films dealt with Russian history while, in Germany, another filmmaker, Fritz Lang (1890–1976), made films that dealt with a society of the future. *Metropolis*, of 1927, shows a nightmare vision of a future world where people are reduced to mechanical robots doing endless, mindless work in industrial factories. The use of powerful, photographic images marks this period in film, still photography and painting, as rich in politically charged art.

Germany, after World War I, was in terrible shape both economically and socially. The economic collapse of Germany on Black Friday in 1927 marked the beginning of the conditions that led to the rise to power of the Nazi Party. The German banks were closed in 1931. A handful of millionaires underwrote the Nazi Party and helped Adolf Hitler come to power in 1933. Hitler suppressed all other political parties and labor unions. Books by non-Nazi or Jewish writers were burned in huge bonfires in the streets. A reign of terror that would soon spread across Europe began in Germany. Three years later, the two Fascist leaders, Hitler and Benito Mussolini of Italy made a pact and formed the Rome–Berlin Axis. On March 15, 1939, Hitler's army invaded Czechoslovakia, on September 1 Germany invaded Poland and two days later World War II began.

One by one, European countries fell to German occupation. On June 14, 1940, the Germans entered Paris. Paris was still the center of the art world with many artists living and working there. However, a number of well known painters and sculptors had fled to New York to escape the Nazis and the devastation of war. Many of the Surrealists left as did Piet Mondrian (1872–1944). But Picasso and a leading member of the Surrealist movement, Joan Miró, remained. Miró had arrived in Paris in 1919 from Spain and made friends with Picasso. He soon met André Masson (1896–1987) who was one of the founders of the Surrealist movement in Paris. In 1925 Miró took part in the Surrealist exhibition that was held in Paris. At this time he was creating costumes and sets for Diaghilev's ballet company. The Surrealists were upset by this use of Miró's Surrealist ideas.

Hitler's Degenerate Art Exhibition_

One of Hitler's first acts upon his rise to power in 1933, was the official suppression of modern art, which he called "degenerate art." He ranted that avant-garde artists were "fools, liars, or criminals who belong in insane asylums or prisons." As a youth, Hitler had aspired to be an artist but he was rejected from the Vienna art academy.

In the summer of 1937, Hitler mounted a large exhibition called *Degenerate Art*. It opened in Munich to large crowds who denounced and ridiculed the art. Works by Kirchner, Nolde, Kandinsky, Picasso, Grosz, Matisse, van Gogh and Chagall, among others, were exhibited with art of the insane. Through his Degenerate Art exhibition Hitler hoped to rid Germany of influences harmful to the nation. Eventually he banned all modern art. Hitler blamed Jewish art critics for fooling the public. He reinstated academic German art as the official art of the German state. While Hitler was busy banning modern art, it is interesting to note that many top officials of the Third Reich were secretly storing the banned art, for their own art collections. ■

Composition *by Joan Miró, painted in the 1940s, shows the artist's distinctive placement of surreal images on a field of color.* ▼

The Theosophical Society

Helena Blavatsky (1831–91) founded the Theosophical Society in 1875 in the United States along with H.S. Olcott and W.Q. Judge. Their aim was to promote universal brotherhood. Theosophists wanted to enhance awareness between nature and the human spirit. These ideas found many followers including Rudolf Steiner (1861–1925) who argued for a view of the world which would bring spiritual freedom.

The Dutch painter Jan Toorop (1858–1928) joined the Theosophical Society in 1909. Around this time, Mondrian joined too. He freely used the symbols of Theosophy in his painting. Iconographic symbols like the cross, triangle, circle, lotus flower and hexagram appear in his work of this period. By 1922 Mondrian became disappointed with the spiritual leadership of the group. ■

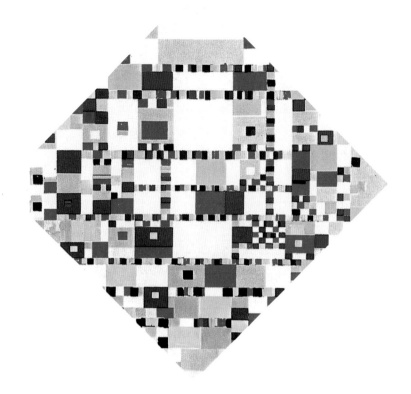

▲ *Piet Mondrian's last painting,* Victory Boogie-Woogie, *painted in oil on canvas in New York in 1943–44, was unfinished at his death. It shows the incredible vitality in his work as he captured the rhythm of the great city.*

▲ *The Frenchman Jean Dubuffet was one of the most imaginative artists working in Europe during the war years. He used the naive style of a child to create this abstract cityscape that is full of energy.* Life Agitated, *painted in 1953, is one of Dubuffet's* Texturologies *in which he used a mix of different processes to apply the paint to make it take on the texture of the earth's soil.*

André Breton's concept of psychic automatism influenced Miró's work as he combined abstract fields of color and line with surreal images. He composed space in his work that is filled with floating shapes and whimsical figures. Small, linear fragments create works full of signs and symbols that combine abstraction with figurative Surrealism. Dots, triangles, blobs and thin black lines floating in space were incorporated into a series of *Blue* paintings made in the 1960s that were completely abstract.

Another artist who worked in the period between the two world wars was Dutch artist Piet Mondrian, one of the most important figures in the development of abstract art. With Theo van Doesburg (1883–1931) he founded Neo-Plasticism and together they launched the magazine *De Stijl* (The Style) in October, 1917, also the name often given to their work. Mondrian was searching for purity of form in his work, reducing what he painted to its elemental shapes and color. He reduced his palette to the primary colors of red, yellow and blue, and black, white and gray. He used a grid comprised of vertical and horizontal lines to structure his paintings. Small rectangles of

▲ *Henry Moore's chalk, pen and watercolor drawings of air-raid shelters in the London Underground like this one entitled* Tube Shelter Perspective, *1941, are like images of the tombs in the Roman catacombs.*

In Two Figures, 1947–48, *carved in elm wood and painted white, Barbara Hepworth used simplified forms to suggest the human body.* ▼

color made the flat design come to life, as the squares and rectangles created a rhythmic pattern. He arrived in the United States in 1940 and his influence on younger artists was immense. Some of his best work was produced in the last two years of his life in New York during the war. *Broadway Boogie-Woogie*, 1942–43, and the unfinished *Victory Boogie-Woogie*, 1944, are perhaps his greatest achievements. They vibrate with the rhythm of the city. They are a visual interpretation of the syncopated music that inspired them.

One of the most interesting artists to come out of the war years was Frenchman Jean Dubuffet (1901–85) who was part of the Art Brut movement. Dubuffet decided to devote his life to art in 1942 when he was forty-one years old. The first Art Brut exhibition took place in 1949. This group of artists believed in crude, raw art that was unrefined or not cultivated. Dubuffet collected the art of amateur or untrained naive painters, the work of the insane and children's art because he said it all was unspoiled and real. A renewed interest in this type of art came about in the late twentieth century and is called Outsider Art.

Dubuffet tried to copy the direct scribblings of these artists and used mixed media to create the gritty realism of his style. Graffiti-like figures were created in thick paint mixed with sand, tar and gravel. He produced some of his finest work in the 1950s in his *Topographies* and in his *Texturologies*. He also created large scale plaster sculpture that retains the playfulness of a child's vision and has been installed in many public spaces throughout the world.

In London, the horrors of the ongoing war were captured in the drawings of British artist Henry Moore (1898–1986) in his *Shelter Drawings*. Moore was an official war artist and these works of 1940 show people huddled for safety in the underground London subway tunnels during bombing raids. The figures are executed in flowing curves that echo the tunnels they inhabit.

After the war, Moore created sculpture of abstract figures. Their curving, organic forms with their hollowed-out spaces look like bones. The figures are stripped of their flesh leaving only a skeletal structure. After 1955, Moore produced seated figures in architectural settings.

Barbara Hepworth (1903–75) was another British sculptor and a contemporary of Moore. She also used hollowed-out forms but her work was even more abstract. It was strongly influenced by the work of Brancusi and Mondrian. After 1934, she began to use geometric forms in her sculpture. She and her husband, the painter Ben Nicholson (1894–1982), moved to the old art colony at St. Ives in Cornwall at the beginning of the war in 1939. After the war, Hepworth took a renewed interest in the figure. In the late 1960s and 1970s, however, she returned to large scale abstraction. She thought that direct carving

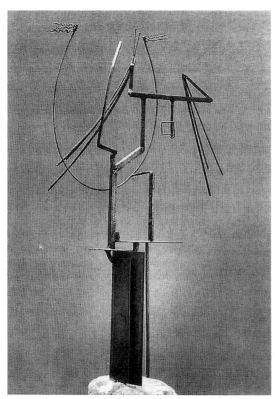

▲ *The beautiful linear elements of Julio Gonzalez's sculpture,* Woman Combing Her Hair, *approx. 1930–33, shows the influence of Picasso. Gonzalez developed a new metal-welding technique that brought a major advance to modern sculpture and influenced many young artists.*

was a "natural and affirmative art." She died in a tragic fire in her studio which is now a museum.

The Spaniard, Julio González (1876–1942) was a leading pioneer in metal sculpture. González used the skills he acquired working as a goldsmith with his father, to make a new kind of welded sculpture. He met Picasso in the 1930s and taught him welding techniques. Picasso, in turn, influenced González's artistic ideas. González used strong linear elements to create flowing movement in hard metal. His work in metal opened the way for contemporary sculpture and particularly the young generation of American and British sculptors who began to work in metal after World War II.

Robert Capa's ▶ *photograph* Loyalist Soldiers Find Time While Preparing for an Attack to Write Letters; During the 1936–37 Campaign (Spanish Civil War) *gives a human face to the war and shows the tragedy of ordinary men.*

Magnum Photo

The Magnum Photo Agency was founded in 1947 in Paris by photographers, Robert Capa, Henri Cartier-Bresson, George Rodger and David Seymour. It was a cooperative of photo-journalists. Their war photographs distinguished this group.

The guiding light of the group was the Hungarian Robert Capa (1913–54). His vivid action scenes of the Spanish Civil War in 1936 included candid shots of soldiers resting or the violence of them being shot. David Seymour (1911–56) was another compassionate war photographer whose pictures of grief-stricken women and children were filled with emotion.

Cartier-Bresson (1908–) photographed Paris and its people. His carefully composed pictures are considered fine art and raised the standards for photo-journalists. ■

▲ *Henri Cartier-Bresson captured a fleeting moment in his photograph* Brussels, 1932, *as two men peer through a mesh wall covering.*

12   The Media and Popular Culture

New York became the world's art capital as World War II caused many artists to leave Europe and settle in the United States. Picasso remained in post-war Paris as did Miró and a host of younger abstract artists, who kept the art scene alive, exciting and important. Some of the old guard abstractionists like Jean Hélion (1904–87) returned from harrowing experiences as prisoners of war and began painting figurative art. But, there was a new group of painters who would take up the challenge of abstraction and produce work of power and expression. This movement was called Tachisme.

Tachisme meant blobs or dabs of color. Tachists opposed geometric abstraction, and created a free Expressionistic style of working. This group is also known as the Art Informal movement. They emphasized intuition and spontaneity in their work. One of its leading painters was Pierre Soulages (1919–) whose strong, black and white paintings were composed of energetic slashing brushstrokes and heavily applied paint. The bold, black lines were like writing, or calligraphy. Soulages's first one-man show was in 1949. He also

Jean Fautrier paints with great spontaneity and rich brushwork. Nude, *1960, is abstract but the loosely sketched form suggests the figure.* ▼

▲ *The strong, slashing, black and white paintings of Pierre Soulages offer a very powerful abstraction, as in this oil on canvas entitled* Painting, *1952.*

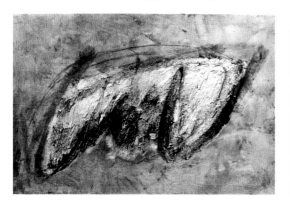

Paris, September 13, 1944_____

Diana Cooper, accompanying her husband to Paris to take up his position as British Ambassador, just a few weeks after the city was liberated, wrote: "...There was little gladness or gaiety in the atmosphere. There were no restaurants or cinemas, no cafes with pavement-tables: lack of electricity, scarcity of food and coffee had dealt with them." ■

Media and Culture___

In the post-World War II era of the late 1950s, Europe made a tremendous comeback economically. With peace and prosperity came a new standard of living. Consumer products were mass-produced and advertising was a new and vital industry. The most important invention of this period was television. Every home owner bought one and the viewer was bombarded with information about new products. The advent of mass communication helped to project a sense of new prosperity. Artists, responding to their world also became caught up in the era of photographic images, television and the new consumer. Some like the Pop artists, began using these commercial images in their paintings. ■

▲ *Alberto Burri uses torn and tattered burlap to recreate his memory of the bandages of the wounded of World War II.* Sacco 4, *1954, is an example of his concern with materials in his work.*

designed stage sets for a number of plays and ballets.

Another important figure in Tachisme was French painter Georges Mathieu (1921–) who worked using paint squeezed from the tube directly onto the canvas. The color was bright and aggressive with no subtleties of tone. Mathieu claimed to be the fastest painter in the world. He often painted before an audience making him one of the early performance artists. He believed that physical action gave his work a direct, immediate expression. Mathieu was also an art critic and his book, *Beyond Tachisme* was published in 1963.

While these artists of the Tachisme group painted abstract images, their work reflected experiences of the war. Jean Fautrier (1898–1964) made a series of paintings during the war entitled *Hostages*. He built-up layers of pastel-colored paint to evoke the horrors and mutilations of the war. Another series called *Nudes* reduced figures to isolated forms within the thick paint. Italian artist Alberto Burri (1915–) was held in a prisoner of war camp in Texas until 1945. He was struck by the bandages of the wounded and, when he returned to Italy after the war, he began to make abstract works of art from cloth soaked in paint. The material took on the aura of blood-stained bandages.

One of the great European abstract artists is the Spaniard Antonio Tàpies (1923–) whose powerful, paintings are poetic and meditative. He developed a mixed media technique in 1953, using fabric, sand, tar and impasto paint. Scratching into the cracked surfaces, Tàpies created a worn look on the surface of his paintings. A 1970 essay by the artist, *Nothing is Mean*, claimed that all materials had validity. Using all types of material, he created collages and large-scale

Spanish painter Antonio Tàpies creates paintings using many materials. The heavily textured surface of Black with Two Lozenges *offers a rich, sensual façade.* ▼

assemblages in which he pulls in the viewer.

In the mid-1950s in England, a new movement sprang up to challenge abstract art. This movement began with the work of Richard Hamilton (1922–). His photo collage in 1956 entitled, *Just What Is It That Makes Today's Homes So Different, So Appealing?* shows a room laden with images of popular culture and the mass media. A muscle-man holds a lollypop as if it was a dumbbell. He first showed this piece in the *This Is Tomorrow* exhibition held at the Whitechapel Art Gallery in London in 1956. Some claim it was the first work of Pop Art to be made.

Commonplace images from the advertising world were elevated to the status of high art by the Pop artists. Pop artists objected to the personal, emotional interior focus of abstract art. Their art was impersonal and took an objective look at contemporary life. They commented on society and the modern, popular culture which took such interest in the everyday world of mass-produced food,

▲ In A Bigger Splash, *painted by David Hockney in 1967, the artist used the images of the southern California lifestyle to create a stark and mysterious image. Hockney, who achieved success in his mid-twenties, is a prolific artist and has experimented with many types of media. He is probably the best known British artist of the post-World War II period.*

▲ *Richard Hamilton's collage* Just What Is It That Makes Today's Homes So Different, So Appealing?, *1956, launched a new art movement in Great Britain that the critic Lawrence Alloway named Pop Art.*

Man in Space_____

The Soviet Union launched its first satellite, Sputnik 1, into outer space on October 4, 1957. With this achievement, the space race began for the superpowers, Russia and the United States. Both countries escalated their space programs to try to be the first to put a man in space. On April 12, 1961, Russia launched Vostok 1 with Cosmonaut Yuri Gagarin aboard. He orbited the earth for an hour and forty-eight minutes. A month later, the United States sent Alan B. Shepherd into space followed by Astronaut John Glenn on February 20, 1962, who orbited the earth three times. As the competition increased, more spectacular feats were attempted and on July 20, 1969, Neil Armstrong took the first steps on the surface of the moon. Artists used photographic images of these flights in their paintings. The photographs of these achievements in space have become powerful icons of the twentieth century. ■

▲ *The performances of Johnny Rotten and Sid Vicious, of the Sex Pistols, had a tremendous influence on young people in the 1970s.*

British Punk

Reacting to the turmoil of the social changes of the 1960s, the British Punk movement exploded in the mid-1970s around Malcolm McLaren's Punk Shop in London. McLaren was connected with the Situationist International group, a loose association of poets, artists and intellectuals who were critical of modern politics and culture. They were very active in the May 1968 riots in Paris and other actions in England and Italy. McLaren helped bring Punk Rock's most famous musical group, the Sex Pistols, together in 1975. The group's members were the singer Johnny Rotten, the guitarist Steve Jones and the bassist Sid Vicious. Their performances were like acts of rebellion. Their rejection of the status quo became a political statement for the subculture of British youth. The clothing designer Vivienne Westwood, McLaren's partner in the Punk Shop, explained what these Punk Rockers were up to. "We were writing on the walls of the Establishment. If you want to find out how much freedom you really have, try making an extreme sexual statement in public." ∎

appliances, machinery and advertisements. While the Pop artists commented on culture, they also embraced all the things they challenged to make their art. The movement took hold in the United States, Great Britain and Canada.

The English artist, David Hockney (1937–) used the flat colors and commercial approach of Pop Art in his figure and landscape paintings but developed a style that moved beyond it. Hockney, like American Pop artist, Andy Warhol became an international art celebrity. His lifestyle is as well known as his work. He has worked in many media. His paintings, drawings, prints, photographs, stage designs and films have had a tremendous influence on modern British art. He is probably the best known British artist of his generation. In the 1990s, his work explored multiple views and spatial break-up, connecting it to Cubism.

The British painter Allen Jones (1937–) also uses the Pop style. He began his career in 1961 when his work was exhibited in the *Young Contemporaries* exhibition in London. His paintings in bright, flat colors are about transformations and the blending of gender. Italian painter Michelangelo Pistelleto (1933–) paints life-size figures on highly polished steel that acts as a mirror. The viewer through the mirror reflection is put into the painting beside the painted figure.

A short-lived movement called Op Art developed in the 1960s. The British painter Bridget Riley (1931–) was one of the major artists who worked in this style. She created abstract optical illusions of space and movement in black and white. The wavy lines she painted seem to undulate and move across the canvas. The patterns vibrate and change shape as the viewer looks at them.

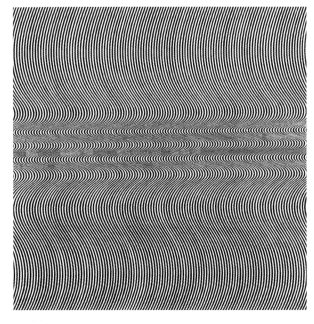

◀ *The Op artist Bridget Riley used rippling lines of synthetic resin paint on composition board to create an optical illusion in* Current, 1964.

13 An Art of the Mind

▲ *Klein asked nude models to roll in paint and press themselves against canvas as musicians played* The Monotone Symphony *composed by the artist.*

Yves Klein

Yves Klein pushed the limits of art to the extreme. To create action paintings he staged happenings that used "live brushes." Nude models were covered with paint. They pressed or rolled their bodies onto canvas creating Klein's *Anthropometries* series, made between 1958 and 1960 and performed in galleries with an audience. ∎

This is Daniel Buren's Piece No. 3 of 1976. ▼

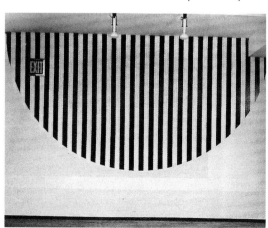

In a retreat from the commercialism of Pop Art, a new movement sprang up in the international art world that eliminated the art object altogether. The movement is called Conceptual Art. It is an art of the mind in which the idea alone is art. Conceptual artists reacted, in part, against the power and commercialism of the galleries. Through text and photographs, they documented their ideas. The photographs took on a new importance as they became, in some cases, the only record of the idea or event.

Around 1957, the French artist Yves Klein (1928–62) began making paintings using only one color. All of his paintings and sculpture from this period were made in a bright, vibrant blue that Klein called IKB—International Klein Blue. In 1958, he held an exhibition, *The Void*, at the Iris Clert Gallery in Paris. The gallery was totally empty and that was the exhibit. This almost caused a riot.

Klein did outrageous things. He served drinks at one of his exhibitions that caused people to have blue urine. His famous photomontage that showed him flying out of his gallery's second floor window was entitled *Leap Into the Void*. He challenged everything about art, the art scene and society in general.

The French artist Daniel Buren (1938–   ) uses a different approach to Conceptual Art. He paints vertical stripes on the walls of museums and galleries that challenge the idea that these are special privileged places. The stripes are usually painted on corners or edges of a room. They are vertical, of one color and 3.4 inches/8.7 centimeters wide.

Jean Tinguely and Kinetic Art

Swiss artist, Jean Tinguely (1925–91) created Kinetic Art or sculpture that moves. Tinguely said that the "only stable thing is movement." His mechanized art is witty and commented on our technological society. His work is often called Junk Sculpture since he used found objects that he assembled into sculptural machines. ∎

This is Jean ▶ *Tinguely's work* Homage to New York, 1960, *just before it blew up in a performance piece.*

Gilbert and ▶
George are seen
as Singing
Sculpture *in this*
1970 work. They
became living art
as they moved
and lipsynced to
a recording.

◀ *This performance*
photograph shows
Joseph Beuys covered
with a felt blanket as a
coyote moves about in
the performance
Coyote: I Like America
and America Likes Me
of 1969.

Arte Povera

Arte Povera uses natural and industrial materials. This art style from Italy united Conceptual art with Earthworks. Artists of this movement felt that the use of certain materials, particularly dirt, undermined the art world's commercialism. ■

▲ *Mario Merz's* Places with No Street, *1987, uses many materials and a primitive igloo to create an environment.*

Few people ▶
actually see
large-scale
earthworks as
most were made
in remote areas.
This photograph
documents
Richard Long's
A Line in
Ireland, *1974.*

Performance art is best seen in the works of Gilbert (1943–) and George (1942–) from Great Britain who say they are "living sculptures." In *Singing Sculpture*, 1970, they stood on a stage and mimed to an old music hall song.

The German artist, Joseph Beuys (1921–86), was one of the leaders of the Fluxus movement founded in Germany in 1962 that opposed tradition and professionalism in the arts. He was one of the most influential artists of the European avant-garde. A pilot in the German airforce during World War II, Beuys was shot down in the Crimea. His Tartar rescuers kept him warm with felt and animal fat. He often used these materials in his work.

Beuys was an intellectual who created installation and performance pieces that were ongoing events. *Coyote*, 1974, was a week-long dialogue with a live coyote in a New York gallery. He wanted to create a revolution in human consciousness through art. Through dialogue and lectures using charts and symbols, he attempted to upset normal routines and common assumptions through his performance art.

Another kind of Conceptual art developed in Europe and the United States. Earthworks took art outside into the landscape. Richard Long (1945–) from Great Britain, made lines, circles, spirals, with rocks, water, wood and mud directly in the landscape. With these he marked his trail, slightly altering the landscape as he moved along it. He documented the event and its aftermath with photographs. Written texts accompany the photos.

The British artist Hamish Fulton (1946–) creates painted sculpture installations and Earthworks. He travels through the landscape, recording his trips with captioned photographs. He frames the pictures with wooden Victorian frames to connect them to nineteenth century expedition photos.

The Spanish artist, Eduardo Chillida (1924–) has created many environments throughout Europe. *Comb of the Winds*, 1985, is placed at the edge of the sea in California. The linear metal sculpture is anchored in the rocks of the coast. The use of water and natural rocks of the landscape creates a work that grows out of nature.

14 A New International Art

▲ *This is Anselm Kiefer's oil on canvas* March Heath, *1974.*

Neo-Expressionist painter Georg Baselitz is known for his upside down figures. In Orange Eater II, *painted in oil on canvas, 1981, Baselitz has painted a person eating an orange upside down, perhaps to suggest that the world is out of control.* ▼

Berlin, Germany was an active artistic center until the rise of Nazism and the devastation of World War II. After the war, German artists felt isolated and alienated from the art world. The building of the Berlin Wall in August, 1961, made the situation much worse. Among other things, it further removed Berlin artists from the European art community.

In the 1980s the German Neo-Expressionist painters called *Neue Wilde* (New Savages) produced work that was lively and expressive. They created a new international art scene in Europe. After the coolness of Conceptual art, this new style of painting offered an emotional and powerful art that used abstract gestural brushwork combined with figurative imagery. This movement proclaimed the end of American dominance of the art market and the beginning of a new international movement that encompassed both New York and Europe.

The exhibition, *Europe '79*, held in Stuttgart, Germany showed the newest trends in art. This show helped to give European artists a renewed status within the international community. Joseph Beuys was the first post-war German artist to receive international recognition. His influence was felt by a host of younger artists, many of whom were his students. Germany had tried to forget its Nazi past. Beuys was an artist who helped to address the issues of the war and to encourage a renewal and healing process through his work.

Anselm Kiefer (1945–) meets the past head on. His first major work in 1969, was a series of black and white photographs of the artist standing in the major cities of Europe that Hitler had occupied entitled *Occupations*. He was photographed giving the Nazi salute. Kiefer believes that for Germany to have a rebirth, Germans must confront the past. He believes that art has healing powers and that the

▲ *This is Francis Bacon's recently discovered* Harlequin, *painted in 1930.*

Lucien Freud's work Naked Man, Back View, *1991–92, is filled with expression. The skin becomes a landscape of rippling flesh. The image is aggressive and disturbing.* ▼

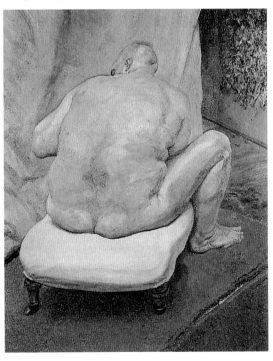

Jorg Immendorf's ▶ Self-Praise Does Not Stink, *1983, shows the interior of a Berlin cafe.*

artist can transform things into something better. Kiefer studied with Beuys for a short time and his work underwent a significant change as a result. He began to use heroic German themes. Many of Kiefer's works are filled with symbols that recall history, myth and German culture. His paintings are large and he freely uses mixed media— paint, straw, poured lead, photographs, wire and tar. His use of materials connects him to a certain symbolism and his past. Kiefer wants no less than a rebirth of the German nation.

The *Zeitgeist* exhibition held in Berlin in 1982 was another important event for European artists because it brought the American and European avant-garde together. Through this exhibition, and others that followed, a new international art market got its start.

Berlin artist Georg Baselitz (1928–) paints large figures and then turns them upside down. By turning the figures on their heads, the artist challenges the viewer's normal way of looking at things. Baselitz wanted to "shake things up" in his art. In the 1960s, two paintings were confiscated by the authorities because they were considered obscene.

Berlin art took many forms. The Fluxus movement, that included Joseph Beuys and Wolf Vostel (1932–) produced photomontages and boxes containing small objects and photos. The work of artist Jörg Immendorf (1945–) is overtly political. His series *Cafe Deutschland*, comments on the division of Germany into two separate states.

In England, Expressionism was much more concerned with psychology. The artist Francis Bacon (1909–92) painted figures filled with pain and terror. Violently painted, they became almost abstract as the artist peeled away their skin to reveal the body interior. Bacon was influenced by Picasso and one of his recently discovered early works, painted at age twenty-one, *Harlequin*, shows his Cubist beginnings.

A New Spirit in Painting, an important exhibition held in London in 1981, included Francis Bacon and Lucien Freud (1922–). Freud never uses professional models, to paint his portraits but asks family and friends to pose for him. The penetrating style of Freud's work gives the viewer a look into the character of the artist's subjects.

55

15 Postmodern Art

Feminist Art

Feminism in the late twentieth century has become a strong voice in art internationally as women have come forward to investigate their roles in society.

From 1973 to 1979 Mary Kelly (1941–) from Great Britain created a video piece called *Post-Partum Document* which analyzed a woman's role in motherhood.

Ulricke Rosenbach (1943–) is an active member of the German Women's movement. She is a performance artist. In 1969, Rosenbach projected slides of images onto her body and videotaped the action. She explores the mythological presentation of women.

Rosemarie Trockel (1952–) of Germany makes universal statements about gender issues in her work. She uses symbols such as the Playboy Bunny logo, the pure-wool seal and other signs. She creates rhythmic, uniform patterns with these common symbols tied to women and their lives. ■

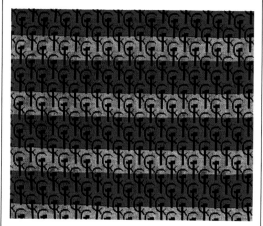

▲ *This is* Untitled, *1986, by Rosemarie Trockel. She uses the universal wool symbol to remind the viewer that women generally work in garment factories.*

▲ Blue Grotto, *1980, by Sandro Chia is a rich blue painting of a cavern in water. A figure dives into the air, bringing a magical touch to the landscape.*

Postmodern art, which matured in the 1980s and 1990s in Europe asks questions about art production and society. These artists returned to figurative work and challenged the notion of avant-garde art. Postmodern artists were no longer outsiders. Many artists had lucrative, professional careers at an early age and enjoyed status and economic rewards. Artists were no longer alienated from society as they had been at other times in European history. Postmodern artists used mass communication and continued to use popular culture in their work. What was innovative one day was often absorbed into the culture the next, as the artists and contemporary society looked for something new over and over again. In Italy a strong figurative style of art developed in the late 1970s to early 1980s called the Transavantgarde. It took different forms in the works of the leading members who included Sandro Chia, Francesco Clemente, Enzo Cucchi and Mimmo Paladino. Transavantgarde artists used a traditional means of expression, usually painting. They generally did not make political statements in their work. Their imagery is expressive, richly colored and sensual and comes from a variety of sources.

Sandro Chia (1946–) paints plump figures engaged in action, usually dancing or flying. Chia's swirling brushwork helps create movement in his paintings. His figures sometimes fall through the sky.

In She and She, *1982 the viewer is left to wonder the meaning of Francesco Clemente's strange figure.*

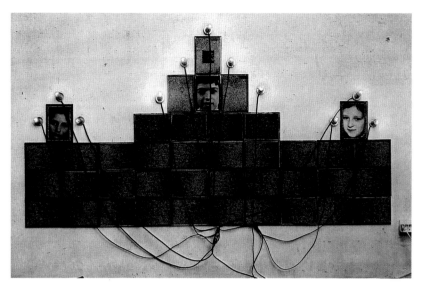

▲ *Christian Boltanski's installation* Monument, *1986, suggests images from a war and of those killed in it.*

▲ *Enzo Cucchi's* A Painting of Precious Fires, *1983, oil on canvas, has a thickly painted surface ringed with small images of fire that is both abstract and figurative.*

This is Bernd and Hilla Becher's document of thirty photographs of water tanks, produced in 1970. ▼

His color is bright and sensual. There is an element of the magical in his work.

The work of Francesco Clemente (1952–) was influenced by Surrealism because he places his figures in strange contexts. There is a complex structure to his work and many layers of meaning in the images he invents. His work is unsettling and the viewer questions what Clemente's paintings are supposed to mean. Clemente lives in Italy, New York and India. He uses many images from Indian culture in his dreamscapes.

Enzo Cucchi (1949–) uses a rich, painterly style to create paintings using symbolic images of fire and water. He makes historical references to places and the past. Mimmo Paladino (1948–) paints in bright, flat colors, placing fragments of figures and other images in a field of color. His imagery suggests pre-history.

The French artist Christian Boltanski (1944–) produces installation pieces. He constructs works that are like altar pieces with boxes containing photographs of faces that are slightly blurred, making them portraits of no particular person. He focuses lights on these installations and the wires from the lamps become linear elements in each work. These works evoke memories of those lost in war and speak quietly of the death of innocent people.

Photography is used in the work of many Postmodern artists. In their collaborative work Hilla (1934–) and Bernd (1931–) Becher use photographs to document architectural structures around the world. They systematically record places and buildings, creating a record of man's imprint on the land. This documentary approach to art presents stark images of water towers, silos and other manmade

57

structures. Gerhard Richter (1932–) uses the photograph as a starting point for his paintings. He paints over family snapshots in an abstract style, often completely covering the photographic image. He also projects a photographic image onto a surface and then paints it realistically, but in a slightly blurred way, like a photograph that is out of focus.

Sculpture is also a lively and exciting medium used by Postmodern artists. Marcel Broodthaers (1929–76), treats everyday objects in an unfamiliar way. There is a sense of mystery in his found object pieces. Polish artist Magdelena Abakanowicz (1930–) makes large woven structures out of rope, sisal and other natural materials. She has produced installations of large, sexless, seated figures. *Backs*, produced in 1982, is a mysterious work that reminds the viewer of the giant figures on Easter Island.

German artist Ulrich Rückriem (1943–) produces stone abstract shapes that he cuts apart and then reassembles. Rebecca Horn (1944–) works with the transformative power of materials like carbon and mercury

Ulrich Rückriem cut and reassembled stone to create Pillar *of 1986.* ▼

▲ *Gerhard Richter paints action paintings in oil on canvas, such as* Untitled, *1984, using photographs as a starting point.*

Magdelena Abakanowicz experimented with rope and other materials in Backs *of 1982.* ▼

Installation Art: Ilya Kabakov

In Installation art an environment is created by an artist. The viewer can enter the environment and experience the work. One of the best examples of Installation art is that of Russian artist Ilya Kabakov (1933–   ). Kabakov's work deals with Communist Russia where contemporary art was forced underground. He criticizes Soviet life and art with humor and inventiveness. In *The Man Who Flew into His Picture*, 1981–88, Kabakov created

◀ *The art of Russian artist Ilya Kabakov is witty and magical. This is* The Man Who Flew into His Picture, *of 1981–88.*

a room with a bare light bulb, a chair and a blank, white wall. The installation has the feeling of an official government room. The white wall looks like a Minimal painting which would have been prohibited in Communist Russia. A closer look shows there is a small silhouette of a man floating in the white, open space. In *The Bridge*, 1992, the artist created a messy room where an exhibit was to take place. In the chaos are tiny paper figures. They add humor and a sense of mystery. Kabakov has created many installations that address his personal life in Communist Russia. While Kabakov's work is critical of official policy toward artists he also takes a warm and affectionate look at that world. ■

which are like a scientific experiment and a kind of performance.

Annette Messager is an artist who combines sculpture, photog_raphy and Installation art. Coming of age during the turbulent late 1960s in Paris, she based her art on philosophical issues. In *The Pikes*, 1991–93, she used parts of dolls, fabric, colored pencil, photographs and metal poles to create a large installation. Almost 200 metal poles impale or support the objects and lean against the wall. This imagery refers to the French Revolution when human heads were impaled on poles. Messager protests against war and violence. The drawings and photos included in the work show people in despair. She is critical of a society that is unable or unwilling to address problems of victimization.

Surfing the Internet

Artists are always searching for new places to show and sell their work. In the 1990s the Internet provided a new international audience and handy information about art and artists. Artist can now market their work through auctions and by direct marketing on the Internet. Current and upcoming exhibitions can be accessed by people all over the world. ■

This installation by Annette Messager, The Pikes, 1991–93, *is made from a variety of objects, photos and drawings. She deals with violence and decay in modern society in her installations. Her work is generally political and visually exciting.* ▼

Bibliography

Cumming, Robert. *Annotated Art*. New York and London: Dorling Kindersley, 1995.

Holt, Elizabeth Gilmore. *The Expanding World of Art, 1874–1902*, Vol. 1. New Haven and London: Yale University Press, 1988.

Jacobs, Michael. *The Good and Simple Life*. Oxford: Phaidon, 1985.

Janson, H.W. *History of Art for Young People*, 4th ed. New York: Harry N. Abrams, 1992.

Jeffrey, Ian. *Photography, A Concise History*. New York and London: Thames and Hudson, 1981.

Kandinsky, Wasily. *Concerning the Spiritual in Art*. Translated by M.T.H. Sadler. New York: Dover Publications, 1977.

Lucie-Smith, Edward. *Movements in Art Since 1945, Issues and Concepts*. New York and London: Oxford University Press, 1995.

Marcus, Greill. *Lipstick Traces, A Secret History of the 20th Century*. Cambridge, Mass.: Harvard University Press, 1989.

Nochlin, Linda. *Women, Art and Power and Other Essays*. New York: Harper and Row, 1988.

Romei, Francesca. *The Story of Sculpture*. Master of Art Series. New York: Peter Bedrick Books, 1995.

Schwarz, Alice, ed. *What The Painter Sees*. New York: Scholastic Books, 1994.

Shattuck, Roger. *The Banquet Years, The Origins of the Avant-Garde in France, 1885 to World War I*. 1955. Garden City, N.Y.: Anchor Books, 1961.

Welton, Jude. *Looking At Art*. Eyewitness Art. New York and London: Dorling Kindersley, 1994.

Yenawine, Philip. *Key Art Terms for Beginners*. New York: Harry N. Abrams, 1995.

Glossary

abstract art Art that does not represent things realistically.

academic art A careful, unspontaneous way of making art that is learned at an art school or academy following precise rules that govern style, subject matter and technique.

avant-garde Art or ideas that are experimental and pioneering.

collage A work of art that combines photographs or other printed images or materials with painted and/or drawn areas.

Cubism An important movement in painting and sculpture in which the object or scene was represented as if the viewer could see it from many perspectives in a single painting, collage or sculpture. Pablo Picasso and Georges Braque were leading artists who worked in this style mainly between approx. 1907 to 1914. This movement is considered one of the turning points in western art.

impasto Paint applied thickly to the canvas or other surface.

Impressionism A painting movement that began in France in the 1860s and which was opposed to academic painting. To capture the immediate visual impression of a subject was the main concern of Impressionist artists.

non-objective Totally abstract and without reference to the external world.

oeuvre An artist's entire body of work.

perspective A way of representing objects or figures in a work of art to show relative distance or depth.

photomontage A composition made up of pictures or parts of pictures, especially photographs.

picture plane The surface of a picture.

plein air The French expression for open air, it describes paintings produced outdoors.

Post-Impressionism Various types of painting that developed after and in reaction to Impressionism particularly in France. Some artists focused on a more scientific way of looking at color, the structure of paintings or the symbolic use of color and line.

Realism Art that depicts things accurately and as they are.

Salons France's annual official art exhibitions, established in 1667.

Surrealism A 1920s and 1930s art movement that started in France and focused on strange and irrational elements in its expression. It grew from the Dada movement. Automatic painting, drawing and writing were some of the activities of the movement's followers who attempted to explore the activities of the unconscious mind. It spread through Europe and finally to the Americas.

ukiyo-e A Japanese term meaning "pictures of the floating world" that describes the prints and paintings produced to capture daily life, particularly in the theater and entertainment district.

Photo Credits

The producers of this book have made every effort to contact all holders of copyrighted works. All copyright holders whom we have been unable to reach are invited to write to Cynthia Parzych Publishing, Inc. so that full acknowledgement may be given in subsequent editions.

Albright-Knox Museum: 25 top left

Art Institute of Chicago: cover, 19 right and bottom left, 28 right, 29 left, 38 bottom left, 39 right

Folkwang Meseum, Essen: 31 top left

Glasgow Art Gallery, 19 top left

Courtesy John Weber Gallery: 52 bottom left

Kröller-Müller Foundation: 25 bottom left

Kunsthalle, Hamburg: 15 bottom

Kunsthalle, Tubingen: 50 left

Los Angeles County Museum of Art: 16 left

Louvre Museum, Paris: 9 bottom left, 10 top, 14 top

Moderna Museet, Stockholm: 47 left

Musée d'Art Moderne, Paris: 42 bottom right, 58 bottom

Musée d'Orsay, Paris: 12 right

Museum of Modern Art, New York: 32, 40 left

National Gallery, London: 24

National Gallery, Oslo: 26 top

National Gallery of Art, Berlin: 40 right, 41 top

National Gallery of Art, Washington, D.C.: 17 left (Chester Dale Collection), 17 right, 18 right

National Gallery of Scotland: 21 left

Philadelphia Museum of Art: 13 left, 27 top left, 34

Phillips Collection, Washington, D.C.: 9 top left

Plymouth Art Gallery: 23 bottom left

Prague Art Museum: 44

Private Collection: 8, 9 right, 10 bottom, 11 top and bottom, 12 left, 13 right, 14 bottom and right, 18 left, 20 top and bottom left, 21 right, 23 top left and right, 25 right, 27 bottom left and right, 28 left, 29 right, 30 left and right, 31 bottom left, 32 left, 33, 35 top and bottom, 36 left, 37 left and right, 38 top left and right, 39 top and bottom left, 41 bottom, 42 left and top right, 43, 45 right, 46 top, 47 top and bottom right, 48 left and right, 49 left and right, 51 right and left, 52 bottom left and right, 53 top, center and bottom left, 54 left, 55 top and bottom left and right, 56 left, 57 top, center and bottom, 57 right, 58 left and top right, 59 left and right

courtesy Ronald Feldman Fine Arts, Inc., New York: 53 right

The Russian Museum, St. Petersburg, 36 right

Sammlung Bruno Bischofberger, Zurich: 56 right

Skagen Museum: 22 left

Sledelijkvan Abbemuseum, Eindhoven: 54 right

Tate Gallery: 22 right, 45 left, 50 right

Tretyakov Gallery, Moscow: 20 right

University of Minnesota, collection of the University Gallery: 46 bottom

Walker Art Center, Minneapolis: 31 right

Yale University Art Gallery: 26 bottom

Index